Heinrich Himmler

Heinrich Himmler

A Photographic Chronicle of Hitler's

Reichsführer-SS

Martin Månsson

Schiffer Military History
Atglen, PA

Dedication

To Mimmi

Book Design by Ian Robertson.

Copyright © 2001 by Martin Månsson.
Library of Congress Catalog Number: 2001089507

Printed in China.
ISBN: 0-7643-1202-2

We are interested in hearing from authors with book ideas on related topics.

Published by Schiffer Publishing Ltd.
4880 Lower Valley Road
Atglen, PA 19310
Phone: (610) 593-1777
FAX: (610) 593-2002
E-mail: Schifferbk@aol.com.
Visit our web site at: www.schifferbooks.com
Please write for a free catalog.
This book may be purchased from the publisher.
Please include $3.95 postage.
Try your bookstore first.

In Europe, Schiffer books are distributed by:
Bushwood Books
6 Marksbury Avenue
Kew Gardens
Surrey TW9 4JF
England
Phone: 44 (0) 20 8392-8585
FAX: 44 (0) 20 8392-9876
E-mail: Bushwd@aol.com.
Free postage in the UK. Europe: air mail at cost.
Try your bookstore first.

Foreword

The passage of time since the end of World War II has seen interest in that influential period ever increasing. A voluminous number off books, many of excellent quality, are ample evidence that all aspects of the conflict are being studied in great detail by a large number of individuals.

Biographical studies abound, particularly pertaining to the significant personalities of Germany's Third Reich. Perhaps no single person creates a more imposing image of authority than Heinrich Himmler. Among the most powerful and influential leaders of the period, his control of the SS and Police, as well as holding other significant posts, has created a mystique around this mild-mannered looking individual.

Attaining his position with a combination of loyalty and diligence, Himmler was only one of the men to lead the SS, but was by far the most influential heads of that organization. Like Hitler, he divided power and authority among his subordinates, retaining his absolute control until the final days of the war. A complicated person, feared, respected and reviled in his time, he was personally responsible for the actions of his command against both Germans and the designated enemies of the Reich. His loyalty to Hitler remained absolute for most of his career and the many branches of the SS evolved into the most powerful branch of the NSDAP under his direction.

An individual obsessed by unusual and sometimes odd beliefs, the fascination with his persona has only increased during the more than five decades since his suicide. This photographic chronicle illustrates the many aspects of Himmler's career. As a researcher and historian on a variety of SS topics, I hope the reader will find this book as visually interesting and informative as I have. My congratulations to the author for his neutral and objective approach to an infamous and fascinating subject.

Mark C. Yerger
June 2000

Introduction

Many books has been written about Heinrich Himmler and the SS. Strangely, no photographic study been assembled. Contained within this volume are several hundred photographs of Himmler, illustrating his entire career from a soldier of the First World War period through the years when he was the second most powerful man in Europe. In the beginning the SS was a small and insignificant organization. At the zenith of the Third Reich, all of Germany was under the controlling influence of Himmler and the SS.

The embryo SS was formed in 1923, during the time of the Munich Beer-hall-putsch. Emil Maurice was entrusted to organize a small unit designated the "Stosstrupp Adolf Hitler." This unit wore the first insignia of the eventual SS. Dressed in their field-gray long coats with the death head on their caps they served as personal protection for Hitler.

The SS was not an impressive organization when Himmler was appointed Reichsführer-SS in 1929. At that time it served under SA command. The SS expanded under Himmler's leadership and continued to grow throughout its entire existence. If Hitler was Germany, Himmler was the SS. Expansion under Himmler's command was enormous and it became the most powerful organization in Germany.

When Hitler was released from prison in 1924, he was even more convinced of his political goals and accepted no question regarding his leadership. The NSDAP had basically collapsed and there were several different factions competing among each other for control. The SA led by former Captain Ernst Röhm still saw Germanys future in its own Brownshirt army. Hitler announced with the reformation of the NSDAP that there would be no more putsches. Power would be obtained by legal means through elections. Hitler would not accept any opposition to this new strategy and one of those who protested most was Ernst Röhm. He thought that his SA should be the basis for the new Germany and refused to let NSDAP officials to issue them orders. Hitler in turn refused to allow the SA to become involved in politics.

In 1924-1925 the conflicts started that later led to the "Night of the Long Knives," during which Röhm and many SA leaders were killed in 1934. The actual birth of the separate SS moved closer. Hitler's longtime friend, Julius Schreck, was appointed in February 1925 to form a new formation with the sole purpose of protecting Hitler. Schreck found his men among those who had earlier served in the "Stosstrupp Adolf Hitler." Schreck was also appointed as the first SS-Führer.

The new SS men wore the same equipment as the SA but with a black tie and death head to differentiate the two organizations. Schreck began to form SS units throughout Germany that consisted of elite groups of 10 men, with none being more than 35 years old. An SS Leader was appointed for each city with the exception of Berlin where 20 men were located with two leaders. Only the most loyal and reliable were selected for the new organization. Meanwhile, Ernst Röhm had fled Germany after a scandal and relocated to Bolivia. His successor was Ernst Pfeffer von Salomon. Himmler was neither the first or the last Reichsführer-SS. Julius Schreck held the senior post initially from formation in February 1925 to April 25, 1926. His successor was Josef Berchtold. Hitler considered von Salomon an effective organizer and granted him free reign in forming new SA units. He also gave him command of the new SS, though von Salomon had little interest in the units. Being an SA leader, he did whatever he could to slow the expansion and influence of the

SS. This resistance forced Berthold to resign and his post was assigned to Erhadt Heiden. Heiden encountered even greater resistance from the SA High Command and was not allowed to form units in areas the SA felt they had insufficient influence or numerical strength.

The men of the new elite remained silent, following their directives that included new rules of conduct initiated by Heiden. People began to take notice of the SS units at NSDAP functions. They were disciplined, their uniforms were impeccable and their obedience to higher authority was absolute. They also behaved far more professionally than the average member of the SA, adding to their image as an elite. Himmler's career began in 1926 as Deputy

SS Leader for Gau "Niederbayern" and the following year he was appointed deputy Reichsführer-SS. When Heiden succumbed to the pressures of the SA High Command, Himmler became Reichsführer-SS on January 6, 1929.

Himmler held the post until the final days of the Third Reich. When word reached Hitler that Himmler was negotiating with the Allies, he was stripped of all his posts and expelled from the NSDAP. Himmler's replacement, Gauleiter Karl Hanke, held the post for little more than a week before the surrender.

This book is not an attempted as a text biography. Rather it is an assembly of Himmler photographs to include information about the various personalities shown with him.

Martin Månsson
Sweden, June 2000

Acknowledgments

Many persons has helped me and contributed with photos and information for this book. It's hard to thank all with only a few words.

Bob Biondi and Peter B. Schiffer: My editor and publisher, without whom this book would not have become a reality.

Mark C. Yerger: Without the help of Mark C. Yerger this book could not have been completed. He has helped from the very beginning, providing encouragement and support. Mark also unselfishly provided photographs and valuable research material. Being the target for most of my questions, our E-Mail exchange could be a book in itself. Mark has been there to reply numerous questions and, despite his own projects, has always taken time for my various needs. His suggestions for improving the text were also appreciated, as well as taking time to write the foreword.

Marc Rikmenspoel: Marc has been one of the largest contributors of photos, his unselfish contribution was invaluable. He also proofread the final manuscript and detected several mistakes. Despite his own research of the Waffen-SS Knight's Cross winners, he took the time to went through all pages of this book. He also offered several valuable ideas and suggestions.

John P. Moore: Whose assistance, especially with computer problems, was deeply appreciated. He unselfishly provided research material, knowledge and interesting information that were very important for this work.

Neill Thomson: One of my oldest friends whose knowledge continues to surprise me. His knowledge of Jochen Peiper and the "LSSAH" is truly remarkable. Even though I have tried to introduce him to the world of computers and to Internet, he has thus far refused. His kindness in allowing me use photos and documents has bettered this work. I still owe you one mate.

MIHAG-CH: A friend I have much to thank for. My appreciation to him for photos and a great deal of assistance in identifying photographs from the SS divisions "Hohenstaufen" and "Götz von Berlichingen."

Patrick Agte: For photos from his book about Jochen Peiper and for much more that does not have anything to do with this project.

David Irving: For letting me use rare photos.

Tommy Natedal: For the use of rare photos, for his wide knowledge and untiring efforts to help me with questions.

Lennart Westberg: My thanks for interesting discussions, advise and for his shared knowledge.

LB: For photos and several interesting discussions. His knowledge and humor is much appreciated.

Holger Thor Nielsen, MIHAG-DK: For a photo and related information.

Erik Rundkvist: For unique photos and documents. His unselfish effort to help with any question was remarkable.

A. Althoff: For unique photos and a lot of help.

Jürgen Weiner: For several nice photos and very interesting information regarding other topics.

Richard Rydén: For rare documents and information about his grandfather SS-Obersturmführer Sven Rydén.

Henrik Lindberg: For photo and instant help with translations.

Christian Habisohn: For several nice and rare photos and his untiring efforts to find more.

Anders Skötte: For rare photos, I hope to see his own work published.

Steve Tashik: For several nice photos and for grammar corrections.

Frank DeLagio: For his assistance with correcting and proofreading. I hope to see your research in print some day.

Russ Goodrich: For checking my grammar. I hope you will visit me again.

Patrick Johnson: For checking my grammar.

Geir Brenden: For a photo and for his unselfish efforts to help in any question I may have.

Jess T. Lukens: For a photo of Michael Wittmann.

Ian Robertson: For designing this book and for his great assistance in the endphase of making this book.

I would also like to thank all those private persons, who for various reasons don't want to be mentioned by name. Your rare photos, assistance and friendship are much appreciated. You know who you are and are not forgotten.

To my wife, daughter, and relatives, who have shared my late nights, high phone bills, and sometimes lack of motivation. Your support has been invaluable. To Napoleon, Lady, and Mimmi, who has changed my office from organized to disorganized chaos.

Cover Photo: Author's Archive

Back Cover Photo: Author's Archive

Heinrich Himmler

7 October 1900 - 23 May 1945

NSDAP Nr: 14 303	**SS Nr: 168**
Member of the NSDAP	August 2, 1923 – April 29, 1945
Member of the SS	February 1925 – April 29, 1945
Gau SS-Führer	1926 – March 1927
Deputy Reichsführer-SS	March 1927 – January 6, 1929
Reichsführer-SS	January 6, 1929 – April 29, 1945
Deputy Commander of the Gestapo in Prussia	April 20, 1934 – June 17, 1936
Commander of the German Police	June 17, 1936 – April 29, 1945
Reich Commissioner of the German Nationhood	October 7, 1939 – April 29, 1945
Head of the RSHA	May 27, 1942 – May 15, 1943
Minister of the Interior	August 25, 1943 – April 29, 1945
Supreme Commander "Heeresgruppe Weichsel"	December 1944 – March 21, 1945
Supreme Commander of the Volksturm	July 21, 1944 – April 29, 1945

Photo of the Himmler family. Heinrich Himmler was the second of three children of Professor Gebhard and his wife Anna. Gebhard Junior was born in 1898, Heinrich Himmler in 1900 and a third brother, Ernst, in 1905. His father was in fact not a Professor even though he held that title. He was an ordinary teacher who for a period was connected with the Royal House of Bavaria. Prince Arnulf of Bavaria, who belonged to the Wittelbach family that ruled southern Germany, assigned Gebhard as a teacher for his son, Prince Heinrich. Later Prince Heinrich of Bavaria agreed to be the godfather of the young Heinrich Himmler who was named after him. (Author's Archive)

Heinrich Himmler as a young schoolboy in an undated photo. (Author's Archive)

A young Heinrich Himmler while still in school. (LB)

A photo showing a young Himmler while still in school during 1919. (LB)

Himmler and Gebhart in 1918. With the connections to the Royal House of Bavaria, there was only one profession for the young Himmler, to be an officer. First he wanted to join the Navy but his sight was too poor. With the help of his father and the Wittelbach family, Heinrich succeeded in being accepted for the army. At the end of 1917 he enlisted for duty with the 11th Infantry Regiment in Bavaria and was sent to an officer candidate course from June 15 until September 15, 1917. Himmler was then sent to a machinegun course that ended on October 1, 1918. The war ended shortly after his graduation and he never saw service at the front. (Author's Archive)

The Himmler family, shown in an undated photo. Both of Himmler's brothers would later serve in the SS. (Author's Archive)

This early photo of Himmler in SS uniform was probably taken in mid 1920s. Note the Swastika armband. (Author's Archive)

Himmler at the barricades during the Beer-hall-putsch in November 1923. After the war he enlisted in a university to study agriculture. In 1919 Himmler arrived at the Technical University in Munich for studies and graduated in 1922. In 1921 he received a note from the military office in Munich that he had been promoted to Fähnrich (sergeant). In January 1922, Himmler met Captain Ernst Röhm for the first time. At Röhm's suggestion, Himmler joined the Freikorps "Reichkriegsflagge" on October 17, 1923. In August that same year, he joined the small NSDAP under the leadership of Adolf Hitler. It was not unusual for veterans of the war to join several different movements. Even though Himmler never saw action he was accepted as a veteran of the war. (Author's Archive)

An early photo showing Gregor Strasser and his secretary, Himmler, outside an NSDAP office. Between Himmler and Strasser is SA-Leader Franz Pfeffer von Salomon. (Author's Archive)

Himmler posing with an SS unit in 1929. (Author's Archive)

An early photo showing Josef Goebbels and Himmler in 1930. They are visiting the formation of the Harzburger Front. Goebbels was born on October 29, 1897, in Rheydt, as the son of a laborer. He tried to join the army in 1914 but was rejected due to a crippled foot and a permanent limp. Goebbels then continued to study at universities in Freiburg, Bonn, Würzburg, Cologne and Munich where his education was financed by a Catholic foundation. He graduated and received the title of Doctor. Goebbels then joined the NSDAP in 1922 and started a journalistic career in the area of Ruhr. He was soon made business manager for the Rhineland Gau and began working for Gregor Strasser and his magazine NS-Briefe. A devotee of Strasser, Goebbels disliked Hitler and once suggested expelling him from the NSDAP. Hitler, who saw the capability in Goebbels, eventually won his trust. From that moment on Goebbels never left his leader. In 1926 Goebbels was appointed Gauleiter of Berlin, a mission he carried out with fanatical energy. He was a very skilled speaker and was also a adept at propaganda. He founded his own newspaper "Der Angriff" and spread his propaganda very effectively. Goebbels realized the importance of using modern technology such as radio and tapes for propaganda purposes. After Hitler's takeover in 1933 there was a special department set up for him, the Ministry of Propaganda. His attempt to control all media in Germany was successful, one element of communication after another fell under his control. He is blamed for "Kristallnacht" when hundreds of Jewish stores and synagogues were damaged or destroyed. During the war, Goebbels was responsible all propaganda directed towards the German people and for the later "Total War" concept. He remained loyal to Hitler through the very end. Hitler's last order to Goebbels was for him to take part in the future government of the Third Reich. That order was the first one he disobeyed. He could not stand living in a Germany without Hitler and decided to commit suicide, taking his family with him. He and his wife Magda killed their six children and then both committed suicide. His wish was to be burned as Hitler had been but the fire was unable to destroy the bodies. The bodies were displayed triumphantly by the Russians when they uncovered the remains for various German soldiers to identify. (David Irving)

Himmler and Röhm attend an SA meeting. Probably taken in Braunschweig during 1931. (Author's Archive)

Heinrich Himmler at a local meeting in 1929, holding the rank as deputy Reichsführer-SS. One of the first duties for the SS was to protect NSDAP leaders at meetings. In this photo they are protecting NSDAP treasurer Franz Xaver Schwartz. The photo was taken in the hometown of Franz Xaver Schwartz, Günzburg. (Author's Archive)

One of the first NSDAP meetings, in February 1925, after Hitler's release from the prison in Landsberg. From left to right are Alfred Rosenberg, Walther Buch, Schwarz, unknown, Hitler, Gregor Strasser and Heinrich Himmler. Himmler served for a period as secretary to Gregor Strasser and undertook his duties when Strasser was otherwise engaged. Hitler formed the SS only a few months after his release from prison and Himmler was the 168th member of this new organization. (Author's Archive)

Himmler, Rudolf Hess, Gregor Strasser, Hitler and SA Chief Pfeffer von Salomon during an SA meeting in 1927. Himmler received more and more responsibility from his leaders. As Strasser's secretary he made his way up in power within the NSDAP. Himmler was now a devoted supporter of Hitler who rewarded his loyalty. It is not known when Himmler met Hitler for the first time. When Strasser traveled in the line of duty, Himmler remained to run the office. In 1925 Himmler was assigned the post of vice district leader, Gauleiter of the Upper-Bavaria area. The same year he also became deputy propaganda leader and in 1927 deputy Reichsführer-SS. (Author's Archive)

A young Heinrich Himmler as Reichsführer-SS in 1929. (Author's Archive)

Himmler in 1933 as Reichsführer-SS. Notice he wears the insignia of an SS-Obergruppenführer. His unique insignia as Reichsführer-SS was issued first in 1934. When Hitler came to power on January 30, 1933, the situation for Himmler did not change. He was not given a high post in the new government and was not asked for his services. Himmler was annoyed that another high SS leader, Kurt Daluege, received a post and became Chief of the Bavarian police. Hermann Göring put Daluege in this position. Göring disliked Himmler and played the two men against each other. Daluege, who was honored by this new title, found out that only Napoleon became a General at an earlier age. Himmler sent one of his young subordinates, SS-Standartenführer Reinhard Heydrich to Berlin with the mission to form some kind of intelligence service and report to Himmler, especially regarding Daluege. Daluege refused Heydrich in his office and sent a note saying that he had spent his time elsewhere. When Heydrich continued his attempts to contact Daluege, a squad from Göring's secret police arrived and threatened Heydrich. He returned to Munich and Himmler. (Author's Archive)

Himmler with his staff in 1933. Next to Himmler's left is Kurt Daluege. "Sepp" Dietrich is at the far right. In the 3rd row stands Reinhard Heydrich, second from right. (Author's Archive)

Himmler and agricultural expert Walter Darré, later Reichs Minister of Agricultural and Affairs, talking to young students in Munich. Himmler had studied agriculture and held this interest for his entire life. It also became a significant aspect of the SS. (Author's Archive)

Himmler and Goebbels at an NSDAP meeting. (David Irving)

The Reichsführer-SS in 1934. Note the collar tabs, the unique insignia that Himmler later wore has not yet been issued. (Author's Archive)

Himmler in 1933 watching soldiers of the SS. (Author's Archive)

From left are: Kurt Daluege, Ernst Röhm and Himmler. The SS-Officer in the background is unknown. (Author's Archive)

An interesting photo showing Ernst Röhm, Himmler and the commander of Hitler's personal bodyguard, the "Leibstandarte-SS Adolf Hitler," Josef "Sepp" Dietrich. While Himmler's SS in 1933 contained 50,000 members, the SA comprised over 400,000 members, more than four times the size of the regular German army. Röhm and several other SA leaders wanted a second revolution in which Germany would become an SA state. Hitler had no intention of granting Röhm's wish and repeatedly pleaded with the SA to remain calm. (Author's Archive)

Himmler, Röhm and Himmler's adjutant Siegfried Seidel-Dittmarsch. The latter also headed a liaison staff of Himmler until his death in 1934. Many of the senior SA leaders were homosexuals, adding embarrassment for the NSDAP leaders. Röhm never hid his interests for young boys. (Mark C. Yerger)

Röhm, Himmler and Siegfried Siedel-Dittmarsch at an SA meeting. (Author's Archive)

Himmler and Röhm inspecting troops. Röhm did not give up the thought of a second revolution and the SA leadership became more and more convinced they were the future of the new Germany. (Author's Archive)

Kurt Daluege, Himmler and Röhm on their way to an SA and SS meeting in 1933. (Author's Archive)

Himmler, Paul Moder and Hans-Adolf Prützmann. Both Moder and Prützmann received high posts within the SS, becoming Higher SS and Police leaders. Both men would also serve in the Waffen-SS. Prützmann was an effective organizer but very brutal. His duty in Russia took more than 360,000 lives. He would later be in command of "Kampfgruppe Prützmann" in Russia, composed of Ordnungspolizei personal. He was awarded the German Cross in Gold for personal bravery. Captured by the British he committed suicide on May 21, 1945. Moder was to hold several posts, mostly civilian. He acted as substitute commander for "Sepp" Dietrich in SS-Oberabschnitt "Spree." Moder later became the SSPF for Warsaw in Poland. He was transferred to the Waffen-SS and the "Totenkopf" Division. Moder was in command of "Kampfgruppe Moder", assembeled from parts of the "Totenkopf" Division as well as army units. He and his group participated in the fight for Demjansk in Russia 1942. In this position Moder and most personnel of his battle group were killed in action near Lake Illmen on February 2, 1942. (Author's Archive)

Heinrich Himmler with an unknown SS-Gruppenführer on his left. On his right is SS-Obersturmbannführer Walter Krüger, later an SS-Obergruppenführer and commander of the Waffen-SS divisions "Das Reich", "Polizei" and the VI.SS-Army-Corps. He was awarded the Swords to his Knight Cross and committed suicide in 1945. The date for this photo is unknown. Note: Between Himmler and Krüger there was a fourth man that has been retouched out of the photo. (Mark C. Yerger)

Himmler having dinner at a hotel in 1933. (Author's Archive)

Himmler and Hermann Göring in Berlin. The photo was taken in 1934. (Author's Archive)

Himmler and Karl Wolff take a rest during the spring of 1934. (A. Althoff)

NSDAP leaders in 1930. From left: Heinrich Himmler, Wilhelm Frick, Hitler, General Ritter von Epp and Hermann Göring. Second row from left: Martin Mutschmann, Joseph Goebbels, Julius Schaub. In the background is Dr. Fritsch. The inner circle around Hitler had begun to form. Nearly all of the men in this photo remained close to Hitler until the end. After the failed putsch in1923, Hitler decided to attack the political system from inside and obtain power by elections. (Author's Archive)

NSDAP leaders after the assumption of power in 1933. From left to right: Julius Streicher, unknown, Wilhelm Frick, Josef Goebbels, Adolf Hitler, Ernst Röhm, Hermann Göring, Kurt Daluege, Heinrich Himmler and Rudolf Hess. (Author's Archive)

*Der kommissarische Polizeipräsident
der Stadt München*

München, den 30. März 1933.

Herrn

B. F u r u g a r d ,

Schweden

Lieber Freund Furugard !

*Für Deine Grüsse besten Dank.
Arbeit gibt es hier entsetzlich viel. Berichte mir
doch einmal wie es bei Euch in Schweden steht.
Dir und Deiner Familie alles Schöne !*

*Heil Hitler !
Dein*

An interesting letter addressed to the Swedish Nazi leader Birger Furugård, who was the leader of the Swedish National Socialist Party (SNSP). The letter is dated March 30, 1933. Note Himmler's title, "Police President of Munich."

Translation:

Dear friend Furugård

Many thanks for your greetings

There is a lot of work here.

Tell me once more what your position is towards us. (The NSDAP) To you and your family all the best

**Heil Hitler
Yours**

**-Signature-
Heinrich Himmler**

(Erik Rundkvist Archive)

Birger Furugård was born in Värmland, Sweden, where he worked as a veterinarian. He led the strongest NS Party in Sweden during the early 1930s. The Party was formed in 1924 and maintained close contacts with the German NSDAP and Adolf Hitler. Many Swedes including Birger Furugård participated in the Party Rally Days of the NSDAP in Nürnberg. Furugård met with Hitler and as a result received financial support from Germany. One of Furugård's closest men, a former Artillery Corporal by the name of Sven-Olof Lindholm, served at the Party HQ in Gothenburg. In 1933 the two separated due to financial arguments and different points of view. On January 14, 1933 Lindholm started a new NS party called National Socialist Workers Party, or NSAP. Many of Swedish NS sympathizers switched allegiance to Lindholm and his party, and Furugård, could do little to stop it. The exodus was so complete that Furugård told the last of his SNSP members to vote for the NSAP in the election of 1935. The NSAP later changed its name to SSS, but after the war it was difficult to continue the party and it was dissolved in 1950.

This picture shows the Swedish NS-Leader Birger Furugård (center) with members of the Swedish Nazi-Party or SNSP. The SNSP had maintained close contact with the German government. The future Swedish Nazi organization, SSS (Swedish-Socialistic Coalition) also had close ties with the NSDAP. (Erik Rundkvist Archive)

Himmler surrounded by SS-Officers. On Himmler's right stands Karl Wolff. The photo was taken sometime between April 20, 1934 and July 4, 1934. (A.Althoff)

Hitler's Berghof in early 1930s. From left are Himmler, Franz Xaver Schwarz and Hitler. Schwarz was one of four who attained the rank of SS-Oberstgruppenführer. (A.Althoff)

Hitler and Himmler are shown at a meeting of the NSDAP in 1933. (Jürgen Weiner)

Röhm and Himmler walk in
the funeral procession for
Siegfried Siedel-Dittmarsch.
(Author's Archive)

February 23, 1934. Himmler, Ernst Röhm and Walter Darré standing in front of the Lutheran Church in Berlin-Schönberg. The coffin in front of them is carrying the body of SS-Gruppenführer Siegfried Seidel-Dittmarsch, Himmler's liaison officer until his death. (Erik Rundkvist Archive)

Hermann Göring receives Himmler's congratulations on his forty-fifth birthday on January 12, 1938. Next in turn are "Sepp" Dietrich and Reinhard Heydrich. Göring held his birthday party at his fabulous residence Carinhall that was built by Swedish architects. The name Carinhall came from Göring's first wife Carin who was from Sweden. Even after Göring remarried Emmy Sonnermann in 1935 he never forgot his first wife who died in 1931. Carin was buried in Sweden, but was brought to Germany and the Carinhall by Göring. The transfer of her remains came by train through Sweden to Göring's residence. When the Russians came close to Carinhall in 1945, Göring destroyed the entire complex. Carin's remains were taken from her coffin and reburied in the woods. She was brought back to her grave in Sweden during the 1950s under her mother's name. (Author's Archive)

Himmler, Karl Wolff and Reinhard Heydrich in Heydrich's new Mercedes-Benz. (Author's Archive)

A historical handshake between Himmler and Göring on April 20, 1934. Here Göring officially turns his Prussian secret police over to Himmler. Called the Gestapa, Geheimestaatspolizeiamt, it was later known as the Gestapo. Göring needed Himmler for to eliminate of Röhm and Himmler wanted the Gestapa. With this handshake, Röhm's fate was sealed. Awakened on the morning of June 30, 1934, Röhm and many high SA-leaders were dragged to prison by the SS. Himmler, Heydrich and Göring planned the operation very carefully. Many of the SA leadership were executed by SS firing squads. (Authors archive)

Hermann Göring, Himmler and Hitler after the "Night of the Long Knives." Note Göring is in SS uniform. As a result of loyalty during the assassination of the SA leadership, the SS was made into an independent organization. (Author's Archive)

Der Reichsparteitag der Arbeit

At the highlight of the Nürnberg party rally, three of the most powerful men in Germany salute their fallen comrades. From left to right are Heinrich Himmler, Adolf Hitler and the new SA chief, Victor Lutze. (Author's Archive)

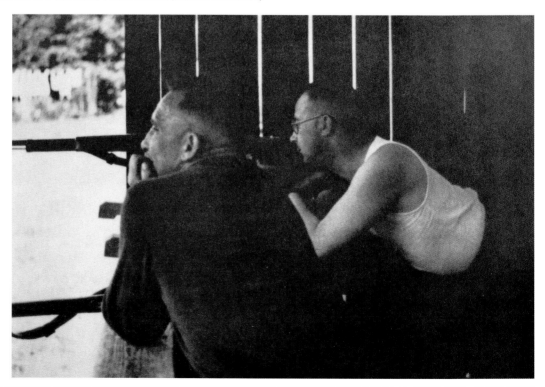

SS members showed their physical capability in qualifying for the SA-Sportabzeichen, the SA-Sport Badge. Even Himmler was forced to do this and this photo shows the Reichsführer-SS in the early 1930s. (Author's Archive)

Himmler reviews his results for the SA-Sportabzeichen. (A.Althoff)

A rare photo showing the Himmler family. This photo was taken at Kassel airport in 1935. Following Himmler and Margarete are Karl Wolff, his wife Frieda and their daughter. Wolff was the long time chief of Himmler's personal staff. He would later hold several different posts within the SS and finally as Höchte SS und Polizeiführer for Italy. (Author's Archive)

Himmler and Karl Wolff in Berlin on December 12, 1933. They are on their way to witness the opening of the Reichstag. (Author's Archive)

From left to right are Josef Goebbels, Himmler, Rudolf Hess, Hitler and Werner von Blomberg. This photo was probably taken in 1934. Von Blomberg was the commander of the armed forces but was out-maneuvered by Hermann Göring and Reinhard Heydrich. He married his long-time secretary who was found to have a past as a prostitute. Von Blomberg also alienated himself when he didn't agree with Hitler's plans for the Sudetenland of Czechoslovakia. When the time was right, Göring and Heydrich presented the color-full material of the Generals new wife. Hitler made the ousting process short and replaced von Blomberg with himself as head of the German armed forces. (David Irving)

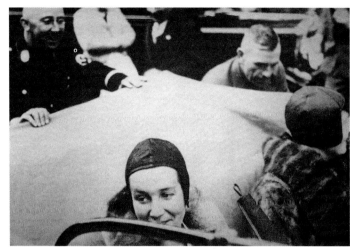

Himmler seems to push the car with Lina Heydrich on the left and Himmler's wife Magda behind the wheel. (Author's Archive)

Himmler and Josef Goebbels. This photo was taken during the Nürnberg Party Rally Days. Note the 1923 Blood Order on Himmler's breast pocket. (Author's Archive)

Heinrich Himmler with his daughter in 1938. (Author's Archive)

Rudolf Hess, Himmler and Hitler at an NSDAP meeting during 1934. (Authors archive)

Hitler consecrating new flags with the Blood Banner from 1923. In the background is Himmler. (Author's Archive)

SS-Obersturmbannführer Ludolf von Alvensleben. This photo was taken in 1934 when von Alvensleben joined the SS. He was born in Halle an der Saale on March 17, 1901. As did many of his peers, he joined the Imperial Army's Prussian Cadet Corps in 1911. Von Alvensleben served most his time in combat during the First World War and when discharged in 1918, continued his service with the Freikorps. In 1920 he decided to return home and worked on his family's estate. In 1923 von Alvensleben joined the Stahlhelm, one of the largest Freikorps. Even though the Stahlhelm had many Nazi's as members, he did not join the NSDAP until 1929. He ended his membership in the Stahlhelm in 1930 and enlisted in the SA in July 1931. He remained with the SA until February 1932 when he joined the SS. On April 1, 1934, von Alvensleben was promoted to SS-Obersturmbannführer and given command of the Dresden based SS-Standarte 46 from April 5, 1934 to September 31, 1935. He was then transferred to SS-Standarte 26 in Halle that had the honor title "Paul Berck." He held this post from October 1, 1934 to September 20, 1936. On April 20, 1936 von Alvensleben was promoted to SS-Standartenführer. On that day von Alvensleben was assigned as commander of the SS-Abschnitt X in Stuttgart and contained the 13th and 63rd Standarten. He held this post until

January 30, 1939. During that time he was promoted to SS-Oberführer effective on January 30, 1937. Even though von Alvensleben was not within the first 100,000 members of the NSDAP, he was awarded the Golden Party Badge on January 30, 1939. Those individuals who had shown intellect and needed skills were sometimes awarded this medal even if they were not within the first 100,000 to join the party. Von Alvensleben held several awards. He received the SA-Sportabzeichen, the Reichsportsabzeichen in Silver and had been given the Totenkopf ring, as well as the SS-Officer's honor sword. From July 1, 1938 to November 14, 1938, he moved on to command SS-Abschnitt XXXIII that was based in Schwerin controlling the 22nd and 74th SS-Standarten. In November 1938 von Alvensleben was appointed chief adjutant to Himmler and held this position during the Polish campaign. He was next appointed to command the "Selbstschutz" in Danzig in October 1939. While at this command, von Alvensleben had one of his relatives shot for sympathizing with the Poles and the Jews. He was responsible for clearing out the Poles and Jews from Danzig area where his methods were rather brutal. He ended this service in December 1939 and enlisted for duty in the Waffen-SS. During the summer of 1940 von Alvensleben was attached to the Regiment "Germania" as SS-Hauptsturmführer der Reserve, even though he held a higher rank in the Allgemeine-SS. The Waffen-SS would even take SS Generals and demote them to field officer rank. He was awarded the Iron Cross second class and the Krim shield for participating in actions in Russia. He left "Germania" and attended a course with the police for other missions. When his studies were completed, he was transferred to the HSSPF "Ost", under SS-Obergruppenführer Friedrich-Wilhelm Krüger. He learned how to run a HSSPF area, "Ost" being one of the most powerful posts which included major parts of the occupied Poland. On October 22, 1941, von Alvensleben was appointed SSPF for the area of "Tschernigow" and became an SS-Brigadeführer. He held this post until November 19, 1941 when Willy Schmelcher replaced him. Von Alvensleben was then appointed SSPF for the "Taurien-Krim-Simferopol" area in Russia. As before with "Tschernigow" he served under the HSSPF "Russland-Süd," SS-Obergruppenführer Hans-Adolf Prützmann. Von Alvensleben held this post until October 6, 1943, when he was transferred to be SSPF "Nikolajew" until February 11, 1944. He was promoted to SS-Gruppenführer on October 9, 1943, and also became a Generalleutnant der Polizei. On July 1, 1944, he was promoted to Generalleutnant der Waffen-SS. From October and December 1943 von Alvensleben was the HSSPF "Schwarzes-Meer." This area was his old "Nikolajew" command that had been developed into a HSSPF area. After being ill for several months, von Alvensleben was appointed to be the HSSPF "Elbe" and also commanded SS-Oberabschnitt "Elbe." His headquarter was placed in Dresden, where he had served before. Taking command effective on February 11, 1944, von Alvensleben spent the rest of the war in this position. When the war was over he went into hiding due to being wanted for war crimes committed during his time as commander of "Selbstschutz Danzig." He escaped to South-America where he lived out the rest of his life. Ludolf von Alvensleben died on March 17, 1970 in Argentina. (Neill Thomson Archive)

This photo of Hermann Göring and Himmler was taken during the Nürnberg Party Rally in 1934. Note that Göring wears the SA uniform. On Göring's shirt pocket hangs the Blutabscheizen, the Blood Order from the beer-hall putsch in 1923. Göring was seriously wounded during the putsch when he was shot in the leg. During his treatment he was given morphine for his pain which later developed into an addiction. Göring escaped to Austria after the putsch where he and his Swedish wife Carin lived at a hotel owned by an NSDAP sympathizer. After a short stay in Italy, Göring and Carin went to Sweden where they lived for several years. Before the putsch, Göring was hired as a civilian pilot in Sweden, during one of his trips he met his future wife Carin von Kantzow. Carin died in 1931 and never saw her husband become the powerful politician of the Third Reich. Göring worshipped Carin and carried her memory with him for rest of his life. His magnificent house outside Berlin was named Carinhall in memory of her. He also named his boat the "Carin II" in her honor. (Jürgen Weiner)

Reinhard Heydrich is shown resting in this prewar photo. Note his chevron for the old fighters of the NSDAP and his sleeve diamond for SD-Membership. Heydrich was born in Halle an der Saale on March 3, 1904. His father, Bruno Heydrich, was the founder of the Halle conservatory and was a good opera singer. His passion for music remained an important part of his life. Heydrich was also a skillful violin and piano player. When he was 15 years old, Heydrich tried to join the Freikorps in Halle but was too young. When the young Heydrich saw the Freikorps in action, fighting the communists, he realized his dream of becoming a military officer. He joined the German navy and in 1922 and was accepted as a cadet. Heydrich served on the battleship "Berlin" where he met future Abwehr commander, Wilhelm Canaris. He was promoted to Unterleutnant and transferred to the battleship "Schleswig-Holstein" where he served as signals officer. During a sailing prom he met a beautiful girl named Lina von Osten. They fell in love and soon they announced their engagement. At that time another girl thought she was engaged to Reinhard. In 1930, Heydrich was taken before a military honor court to explain himself. The court found his conduct did not measure up to naval standards and was expelled from the German navy. Lina von Osten, then a member of the NSDAP, suggested that Heydrich should join as well. An old friend of the family, later SS-Obergruppenführer Friedrich Karl Freiherr von Eberstein, who was the Godfather of Heydrich, helped him by making the necessary contacts. Through his connections in the SS, von Eberstein arranged a meeting between Heydrich and Himmler. At that time, Himmler was searching for someone to form and run a secret service of the SS. He misunderstood the duties Heydrich had in the navy and was under the impression he had worked with naval intelligence. Heydrich was given 20 minutes to write a proposal for the secret service of the SS. Himmler was impressed and Heydrich was accepted. The SD was born. (Author's Archive)

Himmler and Goebbels at the Kroll Opera House in Berlin. The Kroll Opera was used for government meetings before the new Reich Chancellery was done. The old Chancellery was destroyed in the famous fire of 1933. (David Irving)

Three years after Hitler resumed power Himmler was made commander of the entire German Police. In the beginning, Himmler served as Police President in Munich but tried to expand his area of authority. On June 17, 1936, he was appointed commander of the SS and the German Police. This photo shows him giving a speech regarding the new organization. On Himmler's left is the Minister of Interior, Wilhelm Frick, Himmler's formal commander. On Himmler's right stands Kurt Daluege in Police General uniform and Heydrich. (LB)

Himmler (center) holds his SS-Honor sword. Right is Kurt Kaul HSSPF "Südwest." The Standartenführer on Himmler's right is unidentified. This photo was probably taken during 1939 or 1940. (Marc Rikmenspoel)

Himmler at the 1934 NSDAP Party Rally Days in Nürnberg. The SS had expanded and became an independent organization. Note his unique collar tabs that were issued in 1934. (Author's Archive)

Himmler informs his co-workers regarding the new organization and goals of the Police. From left are Heydrich, Himmler, Hans Frank, Dr. Werner Best, Kurt Daluege and Wolf Heinrich Graf (Count) von Helldorf, Police President of Berlin. Hans Frank would later become the commander of General-Government over a portion of occupied Poland. He stood trail in Nürnberg and was executed for war crimes in 1946. Best joined the NSDAP in July 1933 and later became the Landespolizeipräsident in Hessen. He was then transferred to the Gestapo in 1935 and participated in the formation of the SD under Heydrich. Due to his law experience, Best became commander of Amt II of the RSHA in 1939. This department was responsible for questions regarding Organization, Law and Administration. Werner Best later became military commander in France from 1940 to 1942. He was then appointed Reichs Commissioner for Denmark, a post he held until May 1945. A Danish court sentenced him to death but the punishment was commuted to 12 years imprisonment. He was released in 1951 and returned to Germany. In Germany he was accused of being responsible for murders committed in Poland in 1939 but was never able to stand trail due to bad health. (LB)

Karl Wolff, Himmler and Heydrich after the "Night of the Long Knives" in 1934. (LB)

Der Reichsführer-SS
Personalkanzlei
Tgb.Nr. 690/36

Berlin, den 5. März 1936

SS-Standarten-Junker
P e i p e r , Joachim,
SS-Nr. 132 496, SS-Führerschule Braunschweig.

Der Reichsführer-SS hat Sie m.W.v. 25.II.1936 zum

SS-Standarten-Oberjunker

befördert.

Der Personalreferent beim Reichsführer-SS

Schmitt

SS-Brigadeführer

A promotion document for Jochen Peiper, issued during his time at the SS-Junkerschule in Braunschweig. The rank SS-Standarten-Oberjunker was the final cadet rank before graduating as an SS-Officer. Jochen Peiper's final promotion to SS-Standartenführer became effective on January 30, 1945. (Author's Archive)

Himmler and SS-Officers outside the Quedlingburg Cathedral. (Author's Archive)

Himmler with Hans Frank (left) and Robert Ley on right. Both wear political uniforms. Hans Frank became the leader of that part of the occupied Poland called the "General-Government." He was hanged in Nürnberg for war crimes. The SS-Officer on right is SS-Brigadeführer Hans-Friedemann Goetze. (Author's Archive)

Photo from the Quedling cathedral. From left are Martin Bormann, Wilhelm Frick, Kurt Daluege, Himmler and Dr. Robert Ley. Between Himmler and Ley stands Reinhard Heydrich. Wilhelm Frick was one of the most important persons to Hitler during the early days of the NSDAP. He was born on May 12, 1877, the son of a schoolteacher. Due to bad lungs he never fought in the First World War. He studied law and took his doctorate after university studies. Frick was the head of the police section in Munich between 1919 and 1923. When Hitler and the NSDAP contacted the police regarding various permissions for political meetings, it was Frick who was in charge. He became interested in the party and joined the NSDAP in 1922. He and his men were to occupy the police headquarters during the putsch in 1923 but failed. For his role in the putsch he was sentenced to 15 months imprisonment but was soon released and returned to the police. Between 1923 and 1925 Frick was the head of the criminal section of the police in Munich. It is known that he saved Hitler from prosecution several times during the early days. In 1930 was Frick appointed Minister of Interior in Thuringia where the NSDAP had won some seats in the provincial government. When Hitler came to power, Frick was appointed Minister of the Interior for the new Reich, a post he held until 1943 when Himmler replaced him. He was also the man behind the so-called Nürnberg laws against the Jews. He was later prosecuted in the Nürnberg trials and found guilty of war crimes. Wilhelm Frick was hanged on October 16, 1946. (Author's Archive)

Photo of Himmler during his visit to the Quedlingburg Cathedral on July 2, 1936. In this Cathedral the remains of King Heinrich I were buried. On the left are Martin Bormann, Wilhelm Frick and Kurt Daluege. Next to Himmler's right stands Dr. Robert Ley. (Author's Archive)

Himmler at the Quedlingburg Cathedral on July 2, 1936. He gave a speech about the long deceased King Heinrich I. Behind Himmler are, from left, Wilhelm Frick (Minister of the Interior), Kurt Daluege (head of the Orpo), Philipp Bouhler (Business Manager of the NSDAP, later also chief of the Reichs Chancellery), Walther Darré (agricultural expert) and Reinhard Heydrich. Philipp Bouhler was born on September 11, 1899 in Munich. He volunteered for service in the First World War and was badly wounded. He joined the NSDAP in the early days and was close to Hitler. Bouhler was not a man of publicity and very few were aware of his existence. He was one of the earliest co-workers for the National-Socialist magazine "Völkischer Beobachter" under Max Amann. Bouhler was appointed Business Manager of the NSDAP in 1925 and held that post until 1934. As Reichsleiter and deputy for the election district of Westphalia, Bouhler held a post in the Reichstag. He succeeded Heinrich Himmler as police president of Munich in 1934 and was later appointed commander of the Reichs Chancellery in Berlin. To avoid being captured by the Allies, Philipp Bouhler committed suicide in May 1945. (Steve Tashik)

After the speech, Himmler lays a wreath on King Heinrich's grave. He was a devoted admirer of the dead King. (Steve Tashik)

Himmler salutes King Heinrich. Behind Himmler are Karl Wolff, Gauleiter Rudolf Jordan and Reinhard Heydrich. (Steve Tashik)

Himmler participates as witness at the wedding of Richard Prutchnow (SD-Hauptamt). Far left Karl Wolff and, next to Himmler's right, Sigurd Hinrichsen. She would later carry the last name Peiper when she married Jochen Peiper. Far right is Reinhard Heydrich. This photo was taken on January 29, 1937. (Patrick Agte)

Himmler inspects SS-VT troops at SS-Junkerschule "Braunschweig" in 1935. On the left with helmet is the school commander, SS-Standartenführer Paul Hausser. Hausser would later command the SS-Panzer-Division "Das Reich" and was awarded the Knight's Cross with Oakleaves and Swords. (Mark C. Yerger)

Himmler and Joachim von Ribbentrop at the Party Rally days in Nürnberg in 1937. Von Ribbentrop is wearing an SS uniform. Even though he officially was a politico, he held an honorary rank in the SS and a post on Himmler's staff. Von Ribbentrop also wears the chevron of the old fighters of the NSDAP. (Jürgen Weiner)

A photo of Himmler in his office talking on the phone. (A.Althoff)

Himmler, at his desk, reads through papers in 1936. (A.Althoff)

Himmler giving a radio speech on the German Police day, January 28, 1939. (Steve Tashik)

Himmler in Braunschweig during 1936. With a telescope he watches a field exercise. (Author's Archive)

Himmler and the top leaders of the SS and police at a meeting with Hermann Göring in 1937. Note Kurt Daluege in a police general uniform. (Author's Archive)

Opposite: Hitler and Himmler arrive at the "Deutsches Hof" in 1937. (Christian Habisohn)

Himmler is showing Hitler the new police uniforms of 1934. One of Himmler's primary goals was to take control over the entire German police. After Hitler became Germany's leader, Himmler was appointed police commander of Munich. One state after another was then incorporated in Himmler's SS. Germany was divided into different SS areas, SS-Abschnitt (districts) and SS-Oberabschnitt (main districts). (Author's Archive)

Himmler and SS-Obersturm-bannführer Hermann Fegelein in Munich. Fegelein was at that time the commander of the cavalry school in Munich. He would later be the commander of the SS-Kavallerie Division "Florian Geyer." (Author's Archive)

Himmler with his personal staff in 1937. (Author's Archive)

Himmler with the head of RuSHA, Dr. Hermann Reischele. (Marc Rikmenspoel)

Himmler at the martyr monument for the fallen soldiers of the 1923 putsch. This photo was taken on November 9, 1934, the 11th anniversary of the beer hall putsch. Jakob Grimminger holds the blood banner in the background. Note his SA uniform. Every year those killed were honored by the NSDAP. There were two big open halls built at the Feldherrenhalle where those killed were buried. (Author's Archive)

Munich conference on September 29, 1938. Left to right are Hermann Göring, Benito Mussolini, Rudolf Hess, Hitler and Heinrich Himmler. In background behind Mussolini is Victor Lutze, commander of the SA. Behind Hess is Wilhelm Keitel. (Author's Archive)

Himmler at a podium giving a speech during 1943. (Author's Archive)

A photo that originally was in color. It was taken at an NSDAP event before the war. From left are Himmler, Dr. Arthur Seyss-Inquart, Hitler and an NSDAP official. (David Irving)

Himmler attends the winter solstice in December 1938. The Germans call it "Sonnenwende", which translated means the sun turns around. It is an old German tradition that is celebrated even today. (Author's Archive)

March 17, 1938: Hitler and Himmler watching a parade in Vienna. In the background are Walther von Brauschnitz, Erhard Milch and Arthur Seyss-Inquart. Erhard Milch was born in Wilhelmshaven on March 30, 1892. He participated in World War I in the airforce. After the war he held various civil posts within the companies of Junker and Lufthansa. He was to be Hermann Göring's closest co-worker and was later the true leader of the Luftwaffe. Milch participated in the Second World War as commander of Luftflotte V in Norway. After the battle of France, he was promoted to Generaloberst der Luftwaffe and was from 1941 the head of the Air Ministry. He had difficulties with aircraft production and received no support from Göring. Milch lost his posts in the beginning of January 1945 due to arguments with Göring. He was a witness against Göring in Nürnberg. Milch himself was tried in court for war crimes in 1947 and was sentenced to life imprisonment. He was released in 1954 and worked later within the air industry. Erhard Milch died on January 1, 1972 in Wuppertal. (Author's Archive)

Himmler greets Count Ciano, Minister of Foriegn Affairs for Italy. Next to Himmler on his right are Wilhelm Keitel, Gauleiter Bernhard Rust, and Hans Lammers, who wears a rather uncommon sleeveband. The Wehrmacht normally wore this band, which says "Führer Hauptquartier." Hans Lammers served as commander of the guard assigned to the Reich Chancellery. On Himmler's left is Joachim von Ribbentrop, saluting, and Gauleiter Ernst Wilhelm Bouhle. At the far right is Freiherr von Doernberg. (Christian Habisohn/Marc Rikmenspoel)

Left to right are Theodor Eicke, Karl Wolff and Himmler. Theodor Eicke served as the commander of the 10th SS-Standarte based in Neustadt between December 21, 1931 and April 3, 1933. After the occupation of Poland in 1939, he served as the HSSPF (Höhere SS und Polizei Führer) "Ost", from September 10, 1939 to October 1, 1939. Eicke then became the commander of the new SS-Division "Totenkopf" which he commanded until his death on February 26, 1943, when his airplane was shot down. He was awarded the Knight's Cross with Oakleaves while serving as the commander of the "Totenkopf" Division. (Mark C. Yerger)

A pre-war photo originally in color. The SS-Officer on Himmler's left is unknown. On Himmler's right stand Reichsleiter Walter Buch, Gauleiter Adolf Wagner, and Hitler. Wagner participated in the First World War as an officer. He joined the NSDAP in its early years, becoming Gauleiter for Ober-Bayern. In 1936, he was appointed to be Minister of Education and Culture in Bavaria. When the war broke out, Wagner was appointed Reichs Defense Commissioner for the Wehrkreises VII and XIII. (David Irving)

Hitler and Himmler watch a "LSSAH" parade on Hitler's birthday in 1938. (Mark C. Yerger)

Himmler is standing far left in this photo from an NSDAP meeting. Also in the photo are Hitler, Rudolf Hess, Julius Streicher, Julius Schaub and Martin Bormann. (Author's Archive)

Himmler and Heydrich in Vienna during 1938. Hitler, who was born in Austria, had long been obsessed with reuniting Germany and Austria. The NSDAP in Austria worked against the Austrian government where Chancellor Schuschnigg fought in vain to save his country. On March 11, 1938, German troops crossed the border and Austria became "Ostmark", the old German name for the country. Hitler was greeted as the "old son" returning in victory. Himmler and Heydrich had considerable help with building up the SS and SD organization in Austria before the Anschluss. Names like Dr. Ernst Kaltenbrunner, Adolf Eichmann and Arthur Seyss-Inquart created a well working organization by following German directives. Adolf Hitler later described this day as the happiest in his life. (Author's Archive)

Der Reichsführer-SS
Persönlicher Stab

Tgb.Nr.A/pers. *148/58*
Mö/Pa.

Berlin SW 11, den *17* Okt. 38
Prinz-Albrechtstr. 8

Betr.: SS-Untersturmführer Joachim P e i p e r, Pers. Stab RFSS, SS-Nr. 132 496
Bezug: Dort.Schr. v. 30. 6.38 - P. 2/Schl./Wie.

An die
Personalkanzlei RFSS

B e r l i n SW 11

     Der SS-Untersturmführer Joachim P e i p e r, 3. Btl.
der Leibstandarte-SS "Adolf Hitler", wurde mit Wirkung vom
4. Juli 1938 für die Dauer von 3 Monaten zur Dienstleistung
zum Persönlichen Stab RFSS kommandiert. Die Kommandierung ist
am 4. Oktober 1938 abgelaufen.
     Ich bitte, die Kommandierung des SS-Untersturmführers
Peiper auf weitere drei Monate zu verlängern.

Der Stabsführer
des Persönlichen Stabes RFSS

SS-Obersturmbannführer

A document requesting an extension to Jochen Peiper's service as adjutant to Himmler. Peiper was to serve on two separate occasions as Himmler's adjutant. (Author's Archive)

Himmler, Heydrich and Karl Wolff inspecting SS troops in Prague during 1939. (Steve Tashik)

Himmler, Karl Wolff and Reinhard Heydrich. (Author's Archive)

Hitler meets students in Prague in 1939. At the end of 1938, Hitler, with help from Benito Mussolini, got the Sudeten areas of Czechoslovakia. England and France gave into Hitler's demands to control the German areas of Czechoslovakia. In the beginning of 1939, German troops invaded the rest of the country and founded the protectorate Böhmen-Mähren. Himmler and Heydrich stand behind watching. (Author's Archive)

Himmler is giving a speech at the Law Academy in 1935. Seated next to him is Hans Frank, later General-Governor of Poland. He was executed on October 16, 1946. The man on far right is Dr. Werner Best, organizer of the Gestapo. Best held various services in the SS, from 1942 to 1945 he was the head of the German embassy in Copenhagen, Denmark. He was sentenced to death by a Danish court for war crimes but was pardoned in 1951. In 1982, all charges against him were dismissed due to his health. Werner Best died in 1989. (Author's Archive)

Hitler is congratulating new SS officers from "Bad Tölz" and "Braunschweig" in April 20, 1939. Himmler stands in the background. (Author's Archive)

Above, Opposite: Himmler and Hitler at a parade. The SS General between them is Curt von Gottberg who later would be the commander of Kampfgruppe "Von Gottberg." Von Gottberg mostly held civil posts within the SS, but was also engaged in Anti-Partisan operations on the eastern front and was awarded the Bandenkampfabzeichen in Silver. He was also won the Knight's Cross June 30, 1944, for those successful operations. He personally led SS-Kampfgruppe "von Gottberg" that operated in Russia. In August 1944 he was appointed commander of the XII.SS-Armee-Korps. Curt von Gottberg committed suicide on May 9, 1945. (Mark C. Yerger)

Below, Opposite: Himmler, Hermann Göring, Hitler and Curt von Gottberg during a parade. (Mark C. Yerger)

Der Reichsführer-SS
Persönlicher Stab   Berlin, den 19. Januar 1939
Tgb.Nr.Pers. P. 8/39
MÖ/MÜ.

Betrifft: SS-Untersturmführer Joachim P e i p e r , SS-Nr. 132 496, im
         Persönlichen Stab Reichsführer-SS.

Bezug   : Dortiges Schreiben vom 19. Okt.1938.

An die

SS-Personalkanzlei,

B e r l i n .

       Die verlängerte Dienstleistung des SS-Untersturmführers
Joachim P e i p e r beim Persönlichen Stab RFSS ist am
4. Januar 1939 abgelaufen.
       Ich bitte, die Kommandierung des SS-Untersturmführers
Peiper auf ein weiteres Jahr zu verlängern.

                                        Der Stabsführer des
                                        Persönl.Stabes RFSS:

                                        I.V.

                                        — SS-Hauptsturmführer

Document concerning Joachim Peiper's service with Himmler. This document requests a one-year extension of service, ending on January 4, 1939. The request was granted and Peiper continued to serve until May 18, 1940. (Author's Archive)

Himmler watches a parade from his car. (Author's Archive)

Below: Hitler and Himmler inspect the Honor Company of the "LSSAH." (Private Collection)

Himmler and Hitler are watching a parade with soldiers from the "Leibstandarte SS Adolf Hitler." At far right is the commander, Josef "Sepp" Dietrich. Many see this division as the elite's elite. It was a unit with roots from the Putsch in 1923. Originally the "LSSAH" was formed to be Hitler's personal bodyguard but expanded later to an SS Division. "Sepp" Dietrich held command of the "Leibstandarte" until July 1943 when he was transferred to form the I.SS-Panzer-Korps. (Author's Archive)

Himmler presents his birthday gift on Hitler's 50th birthday, April 20, 1939. In background stand "Sepp" Dietrich and Karl Wolff. (Author's Archive)

Heinrich Himmler and his masseur Dr. Felix Kersten. Himmler seems to be airbrushed into the photo. Felix Kersten held a unique post with Himmler, being a Finnish citizen and civilian who had almost unlimited access to the Reichsführer. He was born in Dorpat, Estonia, on September 30, 1898. During the First World War Kersten and his family lost most of their property, which forced them to move to Finland. In 1919, he joined the Finnish army and was promoted to an officer rank. Kersten participated in the Finnish civil war on the "white" side fighting the communists. In 1920 he became a Finnish citizen and planned to make a career in the army. After a serious illness, Kersten was sent to a military hospital for treatment and it was there that he first learned about the art of massage. After studying massage at the university in Helsinki, he moved to Berlin for further studies. Kersten graduated from the University of Berlin in 1921 with a diploma as a masseur. A professor named Binswanger recommended that Kersten visit a Dr. Koo, who was an expert in the art of massage. Dr. Koo was born in China but had grown up in a Tibetan monastery and was educated in the mystic massage profession. Dr. Koo examined Kersten and became interested in the young man. Kersten demonstrated his skills to Dr Koo who told him "My young friend, you know absolutely nothing but I will teach you." After three years of hard study and practice, Dr. Koo was satisfied with the progress his student had made. He gave Kersten his massage practice in Berlin and returned home to China. Kersten now stood alone with a large circle of customers. These included several high industry leaders in Germany. One of them was August Rostberg, General Manager of the mighty Winterhall concern.

He asked Kersten if he wanted to treat Himmler. After some hesitation Kersten agreed to visit Himmler. Himmler suffered from terrible stomach pains from time to time and had found no relief from any German doctor. He had heard about Kersten and Himmler wanted him to try his skills. Kersten lived at this time near Berlin, in Hartzwalde. He also had a house in The Hague where he also had a practice, treating the Royal House of Holland among others. Kersten reported in to the SS guard at Prinz-Albrecht-Strasse Nr.8, one of the most feared addresses in the Third Reich, asking for Himmler personally. After being kept waiting, Kersten was finally led into Himmler's office and the Reichsführer started to explain his pains. Kersten offered very little explanation. He listened through his fingers. Kersten buried his fingers into Himmler's stomach and massaged muscles and nerves. Himmler still suffered from the pain but felt much better when Kersten's treatment was finished. Himmler wanted Kersten to be sworn into the SS with the rank of SS-Standartenführer. Kersten thanked him for the offer but said no. Himmler became a regular customer of Kersten who treated the Reichsführer with great success. As the treatments continued, the more confident Himmler was of his civilian friend. He told Kersten about the up-coming war and the future plans for the Reich. When the war broke out, Kersten's situation became somewhat difficult. The Russians had occupied his former homeland of Estonia and he was sentenced to death for high treason. The Nazis in Holland wanted him dead because of his close relationship with the Royal Family. Since he was a Finnish officer he prepared to return to his homeland and report for service in the army. When the Finnish government found out that Himmler was one of his customers they ordered him to stay close to Himmler and get as much information as he could to pass on. Himmler ordered Kersten to follow him on his field train, "Sonderzug Heinrich." The treatment continued but was never consistent. Kersten never took any payment until the treatment was finished. Himmler was so grateful for his work that he asked him if there was anything he could do in return. August Rostberg, the man who first asked Kersten to treat Himmler, had been sent to a concentration camp for being a social democrat. Kersten asked Himmler to have him freed. Himmler called his secretary, Rudolf Brandt, and told him to give the order to release Rostberg. Kersten's wish was accepted and Rostberg was released. Kersten tried this ploy several times when Himmler suffered from his pains. Most of the time it was successful. Kersten even went up against the Höhere SS und Polizeiführer in Holland, Hanns-Albin Rauter, when he tried to put one of Kersten's friends in prison. With a quick telephone call to Himmler the man was re-leased to Rauter's astonishment. Kersten found a useful helper in Himmler's secretary Rudolf Brandt. He added some names on Kersten's behalf on release documents. Kersten tried to free as many of his old friends from jail as possible. He kept close contact with both the Finnish government and his friends in Holland in order to keep up dated. Reinhard Heydrich once interrogated Kersten and became very suspicious of his actions. Heydrich told Himmler that he would like to know whom Kersten really was and what goals he had. He wanted to arrest Kersten but Himmler disagreed. It all ended with Heydrich telling Kersten that they should meet again, but they never did. Heydrich was sent to Czechoslovakia and later assassinated. In 1943 Kersten was ordered by the Finnish government to come to Finland and give a status report. He was also granted a short visit to Stockholm for a meeting with Swedish government officials. Christian Günther, the Swedish Minister of Foreign Affairs, asked Kersten to use his influence in getting as many Scandinavian concentration camp prisoners freed as was possible. Kersten agreed to do what he could. Together with Günther, the Red Cross and the Swedish State, a plan was drawn up. The Swedish Count Folke Bernadotte, a relative to the Royal House of Sweden, served as the official head of this rescue mission. Kersten's mission was the hardest since he had to get Himmler to agree to the release of several thousand prisoners from the camps. By chance, Kersten was also treating Walter Schellenberg, head of SS Counter Espionage and Gottlob Berger, commander of the SS-Hauptamt. He gained the respect of both men and as the war started to turn against Germany, they agreed to help. Together with the help of Schellenberg, Berger and Rudolf Brandt, Kersten had aligned three very important people who were in key positions on whom he could rely. By the end of 1944, the first transport of prisoners was heading to Sweden as well as 2700 prisoners who otherwise made their way into Switzerland. The so-called "White Busses" from Sweden under Count Folke Bernadotte saved several thousands Scandinavian prisoners. This was a joint effort between Kersten and Himmler that few know about even today. After the war Kersten was deeply involved in the attempt to save Rudolf Brandt's life. He even wrote to the American President Truman with a request to spare his life. All this was in vain and Brandt was executed for war crimes. There was an investigation to try and discover the role Kersten played during the war. The findings resulted in a decoration being presented to him from The Hague. Kersten moved to Stockholm where he lived out the rest of his life. He served as a masseur in France, Germany, Sweden and Holland before a heart attack took his life on April 16, 1960. (LB)

Between the 18th and 22nd of January 1939, Himmler was a guest of the Polish police commander in Warsaw. The next time Himmler visited Poland was seven months later, that time as a conqueror. (Steve Tashik)

This photo of Himmler was taken in August 1939 just before the war broke out. (Author's Archive)

Infanterie an der Front
Deutsche Panzer in Warschau

Kölnische Illustrierte Zeitung

Preis **20** Pfg.
21. September 1939
Nummer 38 / 14. Jahrg.
Druck und Verlag von M.
DuMont Schauberg, Köln

Aufnahme: Friedrich Franz Bauer

Der Führer bespricht die Lage

Unser Bild zeigt ihn mit Reichsführer ҉ Himmler und General der Artillerie von Reichenau

Opposite: Cover from the Cologne Illustrated Magazine showing Hitler with Himmler and artillery General Walter von Reichenau. Between Hitler and Himmler is Martin Bormann. Walter von Reichenau was born on October 8, 1884. He participated in the First World War as battery commander in an artillery regiment and also served as a General Staff Officer. When the war was over he was appointed chief of the Ministry of the Army. Von Reichenau was appointed General-Major on February 1, 1934, General-Lieutenant on October 1, 1935 and full General on October 1, 1936. When the war broke out in 1939, von Reichenau was given command of the 10th Army; the unit he com-

manded during the occupation of Czechoslovakia. In Poland, his army attacked towards Warsaw under Heeresgruppe Süd, commanded by the famous General Gerd von Rundstedt. Shortly after this photo was taken, von Reichenau was promoted to Colonel-General on October 1, 1939. During the battle in west, von Reichenau led the 6th army and fought under Heeresgruppe B in Belgium. On July 19, 1940, he was appointed Generalfeldmarschall. He participated in the attack on Russia and fought with success on the eastern front as commander of the Heeresgruppe Süd. A fatal heart attack ended his life on January 1, 1942. (Christian Habisohn)

A meeting in the Bürgerbräu Keller in 1939. This was the historical place where the Putsch started in November 1923. From left to right are Frank-Josef Huber (Vienna Gestapo chief) Arthur Nebe (commander of the Kripo), Himmler, Heydrich and Heinrich Müller. (Author's Archive)

Himmler, Goebbels, Hess and Martin Bormann listen to a speech by Hitler in Vienna, Austria on April 9, 1938. Bormann was nicknamed "The shadow" because he always followed in Hitler's steps. He was made Secretary of the NSDAP and was also responsible for Hitler's private economy. He was an intriguer who made his way up in the Nazi hierarchy. His fate has never really been solved. He was last seen at the Weidendammer Bridge in Berlin and it is believed that Russians killed him during his attempt to escape. With a skull found at the place where he supposedly died, the identification of Bormann could be made from his old dental cards. His ashes were spread in the Baltic Sea in the fall of 1999. (David Irving)

Himmler and Karl Wolff in white summer uniforms. (Patrick Agte)

A pre-war photo showing the leading Generals of the future war. From left are Alfred Jodl, Wilhelm Keitel, Himmler, and Martin Bormann. Far right is Hitler. Jodl and Keitel were the two who stood by Hitler during the war years. They were both tried and found guilty in the Nürnberg trial and executed for war crimes. (Author's Archive)

Himmler, Hitler and Paul Hausser in 1938. Far right is Himmler's adjutant, Joachim Peiper, who later became one of the most decorated soldiers in the "LSSAH." He became the commander of SS-Panzer-Regiment 1 "LSSAH" and also SS-Kampfgruppe "Peiper." His battles in the Ardennes in 1944 are among the best-documented periods of the entire war. Several books have been written about this combat. Peiper stood trial after the war, accused of murdering American POW's in Malmedy, 1944. He was sentenced to death but the sentence was changed to life imprisonment. (Author's Archive)

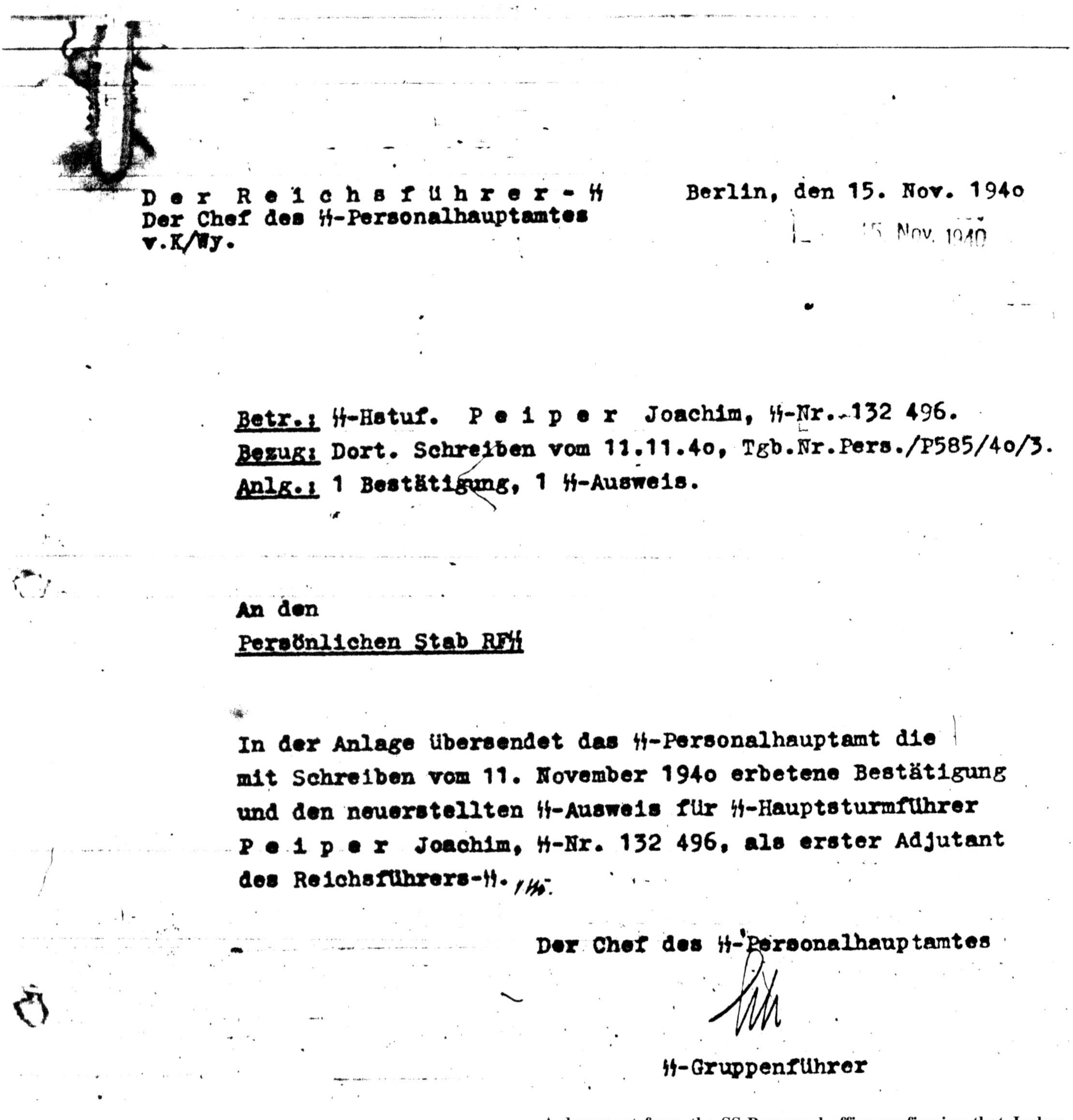

Der Reichsführer - ᛋᛋ   Berlin, den 15. Nov. 1940
Der Chef des ᛋᛋ-Personalhauptamtes
v.K/Wy.   15. Nov. 1940

Betr.: ᛋᛋ-Hstuf. P e i p e r Joachim, ᛋᛋ-Nr. 132 496.
Bezug: Dort. Schreiben vom 11.11.40, Tgb.Nr.Pers./P585/40/3.
Anlg.: 1 Bestätigung, 1 ᛋᛋ-Ausweis.

An den
Persönlichen Stab RFᛋᛋ

In der Anlage übersendet das ᛋᛋ-Personalhauptamt die
mit Schreiben vom 11. November 1940 erbetene Bestätigung
und den neuerstellten ᛋᛋ-Ausweis für ᛋᛋ-Hauptsturmführer
P e i p e r Joachim, ᛋᛋ-Nr. 132 496, als erster Adjutant
des Reichsführers-ᛋᛋ.

                             Der Chef des ᛋᛋ-Personalhauptamtes

                             ᛋᛋ-Gruppenführer

A document from the SS-Personnel office confirming that Jochen Peiper will serve as 1st adjutant to Himmler. This was Peiper's second and final posting as Himmler's adjutant, lasting from June 21, 1940, to August 4, 1941. (Author's Archive)

A photo of Joachim Peiper in 1938 as SS-Obersturmführer. On June 30, 1938, Peiper was appointed as adjutant to Himmler and assumed his new position four days later. Peiper would later become one of the better known soldiers of the Waffen-SS. He also became the highest decorated Panzer leader by winning the Swords to his Knights Cross. Peiper served as Himmler's adjutant between June 30, 1938 and May 18, 1940, then returned to his unit, the 11th Company of the "LSSAH." At that time the "LSSAH" Division was in Belgium engaged in the Western campaign and Peiper was soon awarded the Iron Cross second class, on May 31, 1940. The "LSSAH" continued into France and on June 13, 1940, Peiper was awarded the Iron Cross first class. He was then appointed Kompanieführer for the 11th Company. His time with the "11th" did not last long. On June 21, 1940 Peiper was transferred back to Berlin and once again assigned to Himmler's staff as his adjutant. He accompanied Himmler during his travels, both within and outside of Germany and remained Himmler's adjutant until August 4, 1941. He then returned to the III Battalion of the "LSSAH." Peiper fought with the III Battalion in Russia and Ukraine and on September 14, 1942, was given command of the III Battalion of the SS-Panzer-Grenadier-Regiment 2 "LSSAH." After a short time in France the Division was sent back to the Ukraine and participated in the recapture of Charkow. For his bravery and the progress the III Battalion made, Peiper was awarded the Knights Cross of the Iron Cross. On November 20, 1943, Georg Schönberger, the commander of the SS-Panzer-Regiment 1 "LSSAH", was killed in action. Theodor Wisch, the "LSSAH" Division commander, appointed Peiper as commander of the SS-Panzer-Regiment 1 "LSSAH." Peiper led the regiment through battles in Russia and was soon recognized as a very resourceful and brilliant regiment commander. On January 27, 1944, he was awarded the Oakleaves to his Knights Cross, once again for his tactical prowess in Russia. He was ordered to report to Adolf Hitler's headquarters in Rastenburg and was awarded the Oakleaves personally from Hitler. On June 6, 1944, the Allies started their famous Normandy invasion of France. Peiper and the SS-Panzer-Regiment 1 "LSSAH" were sent to the front where they engaged the British during "Operation Goodwood." They advanced toward Caen while fighting the Canadians. In September 1944, the Division was withdrawn for a short period in preparation for the last large German offensive of the World War II, The Battle of the Ardennes. This battle is one of best documented of the entire war. During the fighting in the Ardennes, U.S. soldiers, who had been taken as prisoners of war, were shot at the Baugnez crossroads near Malmedy. Even though the Ardennes offensive proved unsuccessful for the Germans, Peiper was awarded the Swords to his Knight's Cross. Peiper and the SS-Panzer-Regiment 1 "LSSAH" spent the last days of the war fighting in Austria and eventually surrendered to the Americans. Peiper and some of his men stood later trial for the Malmedy shooting and Peiper was sentenced to death by hanging. He sat in the death cell for several years before the punishment was changed to life-imprisonment. In 1956 Peiper was released and arrived home on December 24, 1956. He began to work for the Porsche motor company in 1957. When it was learned that he was working for Porsche, the company started receiving negative criticism for employing a former war criminal. Because of the bad publicity, Peiper was dismissed. He then went to work for VW, another big motor company who had made Hitler's famous "Volkswagen" cars. He had a couple of peaceful years until 1963 when clouds from his past appeared on the horizon.

When Peiper was stationed in Italy in 1943, he and his command were responsible for destroying a village as reprisal action for a member of his command who was taken hostage by partisans. Their initial mission was to disarm the Italian forces in what was considered a low risk operation. This event became known as "The killing in Boves," for which Peiper was forced to stand trial. The outcome of the trial found nobody guilty due to lack of evidence and Peiper was released after hearing the verdict. This incident terminated his employment with the VW motor company. For a time Peiper for the motor magazine "Auto, Motor und Sport." He soon realized that it was difficult for him to live in Germany so plans were made to move. Peiper found a house in Traves, France. Peiper hoped to get to enjoy the peaceful life he wanted. He was self-employed doing translations. Because he was fluent in English, a motor company requested that he translate a book about Friedrich the Great and Napoleon from English to German. His life was peaceful and without incident until June 22, 1976, when someone painted "PEIPER SS" over one of the roads in Traves. Peiper had never hidden who he was or what he had done. One man, a French communist, had recognized Peiper at a local post-office. Soon a terror campaign against Peiper started. There were articles published in the French left-wing magazine L´Humanité about Peiper which labeled him "The War-Criminal No 1." On the night of July 13, 1976, Peiper's house was set on fire. Peiper, who tried to save important material, was over-come by the smoke and died in his house. To this day, the French police have yet to find those responsible for this crime. His comrades consider Jochen Peiper as the last fallen soldier of the "LSSAH." His body was later returned to Germany and buried in the Peiper family grave. (Neill Thomson Archive)

Himmler with Joachim Peiper in Metz during 1940. (Neill Thomson archive)

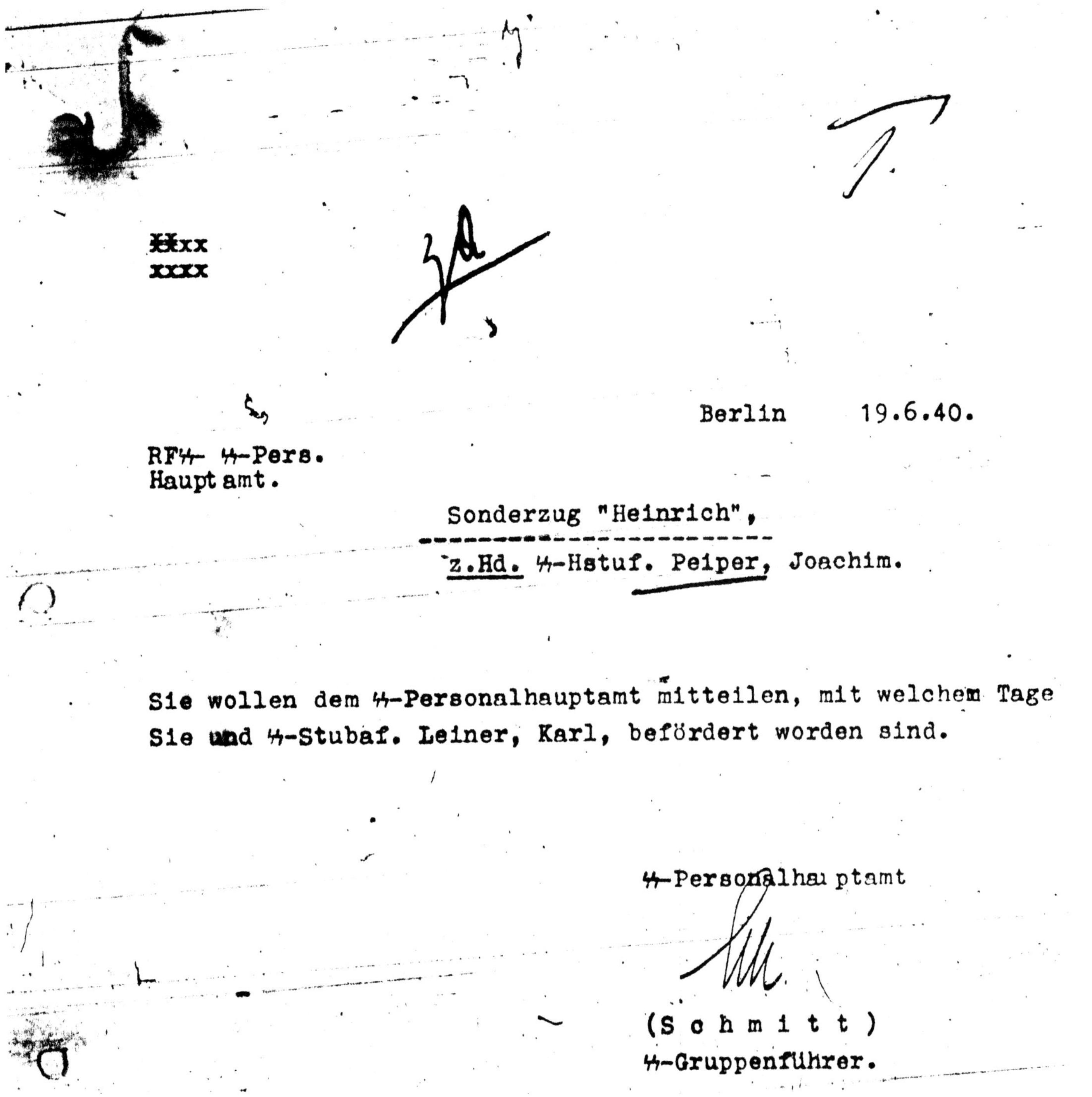

XXxx
XXXX

Berlin   19.6.40.

RFSS- SS-Pers.
Hauptamt.

Sonderzug "Heinrich",
----
z.Hd. SS-Hstuf. Peiper, Joachim.

Sie wollen dem SS-Personalhauptamt mitteilen, mit welchem Tage
Sie und SS-Stubaf. Leiner, Karl, befördert worden sind.

SS-Personalhauptamt

(S c h m i t t)
SS-Gruppenführer.

A document signed by SS-Gruppenführer Walter Schmitt of the SS-
Personalhauptamt. The document is addressed to Peiper on Himmler's
field train "Sonderzug Heinrich." Peiper is asked to enlighten the SS-
Personnel office as to his promotion date to SS-Hauptsturmführer. The
document also requests the last promotion date for SS-
Sturmbannführer Karl Leiner. (Author's Archive)

A relaxed Himmler on a break while traveling. In background is his private train named the "Sonderzug Heinrich." (Author's Archive)

Himmler and Jochen Peiper. (Patrick Agte)

Himmler visits the eastern front in Grodno on June 30, 1941. Standing left in a field coat holding a map is Jochen Peiper. (Patrick Agte)

Himmler with Peiper and an unidentified SS-Officer. (Patrick Agte)

Berlin, den 14. November 1940

An den
SS-Hauptsturmführer

P e i p e r   Joachim
_____

(SS-Nr. 132 496)

Ich ernenne Sie mit Wirkung vom 1. November 1939
zum ersten Adjutanten des Reichsführers-SS.

gez. H. H i m m l e r

F.d.R.

SS-Gruppenführer

1.) Persönlicher Stab RFSS
2.)   "   "   "
3.) Ausweis anbei.

A document addressed to Jochen Peiper, written in Himmler's name and signed by SS-Gruppenführer Walter Schmitt. Himmler appoints Peiper as his 1st adjutant, active from November 1, 1939. (Neill Thomson Archive)

Himmler and Jochen Peiper. (Author's Archive)

Below: "Sepp" Dietrich with Himmler during the 1939 Polish campaign. The attack was a tremendous success that lasted only five weeks. Dietrich was one of the few who dared to take an opposite opinion in discussions with Hitler. One of the long time veterans of the NSDAP, Dietrich participated in the Putsch in 1923 and was the man who raised and first commanded the "LSSAH." He was among one of the most famous Waffen-SS generals. (Author's Archive)

Hitler inspects a destroyed train in Poland in 1939. It took five weeks to conquer Poland using a new military strategy called "Blitzkrieg." Standing behind Hitler are Wilhelm Keitel and Alfred Jodl. At the far right, Heinrich Himmler is shown walking with Martin Bormann. (Author's Archive)

Above, Opposite: Left to right are Paul Hausser, Werner Ostendorff, two unidentified SS-Soldiers and Himmler. This photo was taken in 1940 during an inspection visit to the SS-Division "Reich." (Jürgen Weiner)

Left: Hitler and Himmler are probably at a field HQ. The photo was taken in France during June 1940. Note the white markings on the trees. They were used for orientation at night. (Gary Wood)

Himmler speaking to the "Das Reich" commander Paul Hausser. Far right is "Deutschland" commander Heinz Harmel. Harmel was to command the SS-Panzer-Division "Frundsberg." Harmel joined the SS-VT in 1935 and served in the SS-Regiment "Germania", that later became a part of the SS-Division "Wiking." He participated in the invasions of Poland and France. He was awarded both classes of the Iron Cross for battles in the West. Assigned to SS-Regiment "Deutschland" as commander, Harmel was awarded the Knight's Cross for his bravery during the fighting against the Russia. Harmel was also awarded the Oakleaves to his Knight's Cross in 1943 during the fighting in Russia. After a period in a hospital when wounded, Harmel was sent to a Divisional Commanders course from which he graduated. He was assigned the command of the 10.SS-Panzer-Division "Frundsberg" on April 27, 1944. His division fought against the allied parachutists in Arnhem, Holland under SS Corps commander Wilhelm Bittrich. As commander of the "Frundsberg" Division, Harmel was awarded the swords to his Knight's Cross on November 28, 1944. Heinz Harmel died on September 2, 2000. (Marc Rikmenspoel)

Himmler, SS-Gruppenführer Paul Hausser and Karl Wolff. Hausser was the first to receive the rank of SS-Oberstgruppenführer of the Waffen-SS on April 20, 1944. The other Waffen-SS general who reached this rank was "Sepp" Dietrich. (Author's Archive)

Himmler on a field inspection to "Das Reich." (Author's Archive)

Himmler pays a visit to the "Das Reich" Division. On the right the division commander Walter Krüger is seen. (Mark Rikmenspoel)

Martin Bormann, Karl Wolff, Himmler and Jochen Peiper. Adolf Hitler is in the front row of a parade. (Patrick Agte)

Above, Opposite: Himmler congratulates Gerd Pleiss on his Knight's Cross. Pleiss received the decoration on April 20, 1941, as SS-Obersturmführer and commander of the 1st Company of "Leibstandarte SS Adolf Hitler." Next to Pleiss stands Max Hansen, later commander of SS-Panzer-Grenadier-Regiment 1 "LSSAH." To the far left is Rudolf Lehmann, later commander of the "Das Reich" Division. During the attack on Rostow, Russia, Pleiss stepped on a mine and lost both of his both legs. On the way to the field hospital he died on November 17, 1941. (Marc Rikmenspoel)

Below, Opposite: Himmler and "Sepp" Dietrich salute the "Leibstandarte" Division. This photo was taken after the ceremony for the new banner of the "Leibstandarte" in Metz. (Author's Archive)

Above: "Sepp" Dietrich gives a speech after the ceremony for the newly issued banner of the Leibstandarte. The normal banner of this kind contained the text "Deutschland Erwache" (Germany awake). Due to its special status, the "LSSAH" held received this unique banner. (Author's Archive)

Kurt "Panzermeyer" Meyer watches Himmler while talking to one of his friends of the "LSSAH" division. "Panzermeyer" is one of the best known Waffen-SS officers. His excellent book "Grenadiers" has sold several thousand of copies and tells a remarkable story. Kurt Meyer was born on December 23, 1910 in Jerxheim. He joined the Hitlerjugend in 1925 and then the SA in 1928. Meyer left the SA in 1930 and transferred to the SS in 1931. He was placed in the 22.SS-Standarte and served there until 1934 when he joined the "Leibstandarte." Meyer participated in the Polish campaign and was awarded the Iron Cross Second Class. Then transferred to the SS-Kradschützen-Kompanie of the "LSSAH" as commander, he fought with success in the West and won the Iron Cross First Class. Kurt Meyer was then assigned to the SS-Aufklärungs-Abteilung 1 "LSSAH" as commander and was nicknamed "Schnelle Meyer" (speedy Meyer) due to his quickly advancing way of action. A very skillful and competent leader, he was awarded several high decorations starting with the Knight's Cross on May 18, 1941 during the campaign in Greece. That was followed by the German Cross in Gold on February 8, 1942 during the battles in Russia. He was later also awarded the Oakleaves to his Knight's Cross as the commander of the SS-Aufklärungs-Abteilung 1 "LSSAH." When the new SS-Division "Hitlerjugend" was formed, Meyer was reassigned and became the commander of SS-Panzer-Grenadier-Regiment 25. When divisional commander Fritz Witt was killed by naval gunfire, Meyer was proposed by "Sepp" Dietrich to assume command of the division. Meyer, now called "Panzermeyer," led the Hitlerjugend Division at the Western front and was awarded the Swords to his Knight's Cross on August 27, 1944. He was taken prisoner by Belgian partisans on September 6, 1944 and handed over to the British. Meyer was sent to England where he met Max Wünsche, a longtime friend

and his former regimental commander of the SS-Panzer-Regiment 12. Meyer was tried in a Canadian court for the killing of Canadian soldiers. He was sentenced to death and brought to Canada. There were several protests against his punishment and several higher West German officials petitioned for his release. Meyer was released on September 6, 1954 and returned home to his family. His old nickname "Schnelle Meyer" continued as he made untiring attempts for all the former Waffen-SS soldiers to be treated as regular soldiers of the German army. The court in Nürnberg had named the entire SS organization, including the Waffen-SS, a criminal organization. His personal efforts would cost him his life. On his 51st birthday on December 23, 1961, he suffered from a fatal heart attack and one of the most legendary soldiers of the Waffen-SS died. He was followed to his final resting place by thousands of former Waffen-SS soldiers. (Marc Rikmenspoel)

Above, Opposite: Himmler pays a visit to the first SS-Panzer-Division "Leibstandarte SS Adolf Hitler." Himmler speaks to division commander "Sepp" Dietrich. On right in black Panzer uniform is Georg Schönberger, commander of the SS-Panzer Regiment 1 "LSSAH." He first led the SS-Sturmgeschütz-Abteilung "LSSAH" and was then assigned the SS-Panzer-Abteilung 1 where he took over the command from Wilhelm Mohnke. Schönberger was awarded the German Cross in Gold and posthumously the Knight's Cross. He was killed in action on November 20, 1943 in Russia and was also promoted posthumously to SS-Standartenführer. (Marc Rikmenspoel)

Below, Opposite: Himmler studies a 5cm anti-tank gun with "Sepp" Dietrich and Karl Wolff. Far right stands Himmler's adjutant, Werner Grothmann. (Patrick Agte)

Himmler and "Sepp" Dietrich, the commander of the 1. SS-Panzer-Division "Leibstandarte SS Adolf Hitler." Dietrich had a tremendous career in the SS and became a successful divisional commander during the war. One of four who held the rank of SS-Oberstgruppenführer, he was also awarded the Diamonds to the Knights Cross for his successful leadership. (Patrick Agte)

At a field quarters in Thessaly are Fritz Witt, Himmler and Peiper. Fritz Witt was one of the 120 original members who formed the "Leibstandarte" under the command of "Sepp" Dietrich. He joined SS-Standarte "Deutschland" as a company commander in 1935, under Battalion commander Felix Steiner. Witt went to war with "Deutschland" and participated in the Polish campaign where he won both classes of the Iron Cross. During the war in France he was awarded the Knights Cross as the commander of I./Deutschland. Returning to the "Leibstandarte," he fought in the Balkans and in Russia. He won the Oakleaves to his Knights Cross in 1943 as the commander of SS-Panzer-Grenadier Regiment 1, "LSSAH." He was appointed the command for the newly formed "Hitlerjugend" Division, training and developed the division for coming battles. During a calm day at the Normandy front playing cards with his orderly officer and other staff members of the division, a ship's artillery shell found its way to the place where Witt and his friends sat. It was a direct hit that killed Witt and his friends on June 16, 1944. His grave can be seen at the German War Cemetery at Champigny, France. (Patrick Agte)

Himmler pays a visit to the "Leibstandarte" in Greece on May 9, 1941. Left to Right: Max Wünsche, "Sepp" Dietrich, Himmler, Karl Wolff, Jochen Peiper and Fritz Witt. (Patrick Agte)

Below: Himmler talks to an unidentified SS general, behind him is Peiper. (Patrick Agte)

Himmler visits a Russian T-34 tank factory on the Russian front. Next to Himmler is "Sepp" Dietrich. To the far right, in a black Panzer uniform, is Georg Schönberger. (MIHAG-CH)

Himmler with his staff rests in the newly founded General-Government of former Poland in October 1939. Peiper is at left and on the right is Karl Wolff. (Patrick Agte)

Himmler having a conversation with "Sepp" Dietrich. (Marc Rikmenspoel)

Left to right are Joachim Peiper, "Sepp" Dietrich and Heinrich Himmler inspecting troops of the "Leibstandarte" during 1940. Joachim Peiper was twice adjutant to Himmler. He was very well liked by Himmler who wrote following Peiper's award of the Knight's Cross: "Dear Jochen, warmest greetings for the Knight's Cross, your Heinrich Himmler." Peiper would later be awarded the Swords to the Knight's Cross and also won the German Cross in Gold. His life ended in a tragedy. French communists set Peiper's house on fire in Traves. To this day no one has been found guilty of the murder. (Neill Thomson archive)

Greece in 1941. From left are Fritz Witt (on his knees), Heinrich Springer, "Sepp" Dietrich, Jochen Peiper (Himmler's adjutant), Max Wünsche, Werner Grothmann, (Himmler's 2nd adjutant), an unknown SS-Untersturmführer and Himmler. Fritz Witt is explaining one of the actions taking place during the battle. Heinrich Springer was born on November 3, 1914 in Kiel. As a youth he joined the Hitlerjugend and enlisted in the SS in 1937. Springer was ordered to report to the SS-Standarte "Germania" and after one year was sent to SS-Junkerschule "Tölz" for officer training. After his graduation, Springer came to the "LSSAH" as Zugführer (platoon leader). He was appointed commander of the 3rd Company of the "LSSAH" and saw action on the Eastern Front. Springer was awarded the Knights Cross on January 12, 1942, as an SS-Hauptsturmführer and commander of the 3rd Company for capturing the key bridge across the Don River in Rostov. In 1943, Springer was assigned to the SS-Division "Hitlerjugend" as the divisional adjutant. He was reassigned to Heeresgruppe B as an orderly officer near the end of the war. During the last days, the commander for Heeresgruppe B, Field Marshal Walter Model received a request from Himmler for the transfer of Springer to his staff. Model accommodated Himmler's wish and Springer was transferred where he served as the orderly officer to Himmler until the war ended. (Neill Thomson Archive)

SS-Obersturmbannführer Max Wünsche is giving Hitler a gift from the I.SS-Panzer-Korps on his birthday, April 20, 1944, while Himmler is watching. Max Wünsche was born on April 20, 1914 in Kittlitz. He studied in a higher business school and graduated with good reports. He became a section manager at a small bookkeeping company in his hometown. Wünsche joined the Hitlerjugend in 1932 and in 1933 accepted into the SS. He soon became an NCO and unit commander. He impressed his commanders and higher officers with his skill and they recommended him to attend SS-Junkerschule to become an officer. Wünsche went to SS-Junkerschule "Tölz" on April 25, 1935, and graduated in January 1936 as an SS-Standartenjunker. His commission was received on the birthday he shared with Hitler, April 20 1936. Wünsche was assigned to the 9.Sturm of the "LSSAH." At that time the "LSSAH" was not composed of regiments. Wünsche was soon transferred to the 11.Sturm of the "LSSAH" and he held a position as Zugführer. In September of 1938, Wünsche was transferred to the Führer-Begleit-Kommando and was soon to serve as adjutant to Hitler. Wünsche can be seen in several photo's and news films during that time. Wünsche ended his time as adjutant to Hitler on January 24, 1940, and went to the 15.Sturm of the "LSSAH." He was soon transferred again and went to the SS-Kradschützen-Abteilung 1 under later division commander Kurt "Panzermeyer" Meyer. During the battles in the West through Holland, Belgium and France, Wünsche was awarded with both classes of the Iron Cross. On June 1, 1940, he returned to the Hitler's staff and served once again as his adjutant. This service lasted until December 5, 1940, when he went to the divisional staff of the "LSSAH." He was to serve as adjutant for commander "Sepp" Dietrich until February 1942. Wünsche was then transferred to the SS-Sturmgeschütz-Abteilung of the "LSSAH" and became its commander. On October 22, 1942, Wünsche transferred to SS-Panzer-Regiment 1 under the command of Georg Schönberger. Wünsche was appointed commander of the I.Abteilung and was initially sent to France where the division was stationed for occupation duties. In early 1943, Wünsche and the division went to Russia and participated in the recapture of Charkow. During this campaign, "Panzermeyer" led a small Kampfgruppe that was encircled by Russian troops. Their situation became more and more chaotic. Wünsche led a small group of men trying to rescue Meyer and his men, including the son of Joachim von Ribbentrop, Rudolf von Ribbentrop, who at that time was seriously wounded. The entire division fought against the Russian encirclement and Wünsche's group was among the first to assist "Panzermeyer." Wünsche was later won the German Cross in Gold for his personal bravery in combat and awarded the Knight's Cross on February 28, 1943. Wünsche's unit destroyed more than 50 Soviet cannons and one German tank by mistake. The group lost 5 men and 14 were wounded while the Russians counted over 800 dead. Wünsche was not the only one in the group who was awarded the Knight's Cross, SS-Oberscharführer Hans Riemling received it at the same time for his participation and bravery in combat. In the beginning of 1943, Wünsche was informed that a new SS-Panzer-Division would be formed and he was assigned to be the new commander of SS-Panzer-Regiment 12 "Hitlerjugend." The "Hitlerjugend" Division can be called the sister division of the "LSSAH." Many higher officers including Wünsche, Fritz Witt and "Panzermeyer" were transferred to the new division. Wünsche and his officers formed the new regiment that later fought with success in the battle of Normandy in 1944. Wünsche was awarded the Oakleaves to his Knight's Cross on August 11, 1944, as result of the success of the unit and his bravery. On August 21, 1944, the situation became very dangerous when Wünsche and two other regimental staff officers were cut of from their own lines. Wünsche and his men were on their own for four days in enemy territory before they were caught. Before they were taken prisoners they had removed all SS-Insignia from their uniforms and dressed in Luftwaffe uniforms. However, Wünsche was identified as Max Wünsche, SS-Obersturmbannführer and commander of SS-Panzer-Regiment 12. He met the legendary Field Marshal Montgomery who told Wünsche that he would not be treated according to the Geneva Convention, just because of his membership in the SS. Wünsche was sent to England as a POW and was released in 1948. He then had a civil career as a businessman and had six sons with his wife. Wünsche kept close contact with his friends from the war until he passed away on April 17, 1995. (Author's Archive)

Georg Schönberger, "Sepp" Dietrich and Himmler in Charkow, Ukraine. Schönberger was the first commander of SS-Panzer-Regiment 1 "LSSAH." He was awarded the German Cross in Gold and, posthumously, the Knight's Cross. He was killed in action on November 20, 1943, in Russia. He was replaced with Himmler's former adjutant, Joachim Peiper. In this photo Schönberger is showing a Russian T-34. (Mark C. Yerger)

Karl Wolff, Joachim Peiper, "Sepp" Dietrich and Himmler inspecting troops in Greece during 1941. (Neill Thomson archive)

Himmler visits the SS-Panzer-Korps and Georg Schönberger. On his left is "Sepp" Dietrich. (Mark C. Yerger)

Himmler and "Sepp" Dietrich, commander of the SS-Division "Leibstandarte SS Adolf Hitler." Dietrich was to command the first SS-Division until July 1943 when SS-Standartenführer Theodor Wisch replaced him. Dietrich's next command the I/SS-Panzer-Korps, which he commanded until October 1944. Dietrich later commanded the 5.Panzer-Armee and finally the 6.SS-Panzer-Armee. (Mark C. Yerger)

Wewelsburg castle, where Himmler founded the home of his black order. There are many stories about the library containing several thousand books concerning race development. Himmler created a special "hall of fame", the Obergruppenführersaal, similar to King Arthur's round table. The crypt of the castle contained 12 small pedestals where the urns of the highest SS leaders of the Reich would rest. The only light in the crypt was from a small light inlet in the vault roof that was decorated with a large swastika. (Author's Archive)

Himmler speaks with Hermann Bartels, in civilian clothes. Behind Bartels stands Heydrich. The SS General at far right is Karl-Maria Willigut-Weisthor. Bartels served for a period on the Himmler's staff. Karl-Maria Willigut-Weisthor is one of the most mysterious SS Generals. Born in Vienna on December 10, 1866, he joined the Austrian army in 1884, fighting in the First World War on the Eastern and Italian fronts. Willigut was from his early years obsessed with the Germanic folklore, and when he left the army in 1919, his interest intensified. After a wrecked marriage, Willigut was placed in a mental hospital for depression, remaining there between the years of 1924 and 1927. He immigrated to Germany in 1932 and met an old friend, Richard Anders. Anders was involved in a mystic lodge called "Ordo Novi Templi." Richard Anders probably introduced Willigut to Himmler, who, like Willigut, was very interested in Germanic folklore. Willigut was accepted into the SS, but under the name of Karl Weisthor. He received the rank of SS-Untersturmführer on February 1, 1932. He was attached to Himmler's staff and later went to the historical research department of the SS, later part of RSHA. Willigut-Weisthor is likely the man who designed the famous Totenkopf Ring and also the man who brought Wewelsburg castle to Himmler's attention. During 1938-1939, Willigut's health declined. Eventually, his old mental problems showed up again. He was forced to leave the SS, being forced return all SS insignia, such as the Totenkopf ring, SS dagger and SS sword. His resignation is dated August 28, 1939. He remained under the eyes of the SS who helped him in getting a personal assistant. In 1943 Willigut moved to an SS guest house in Carinthia, Austria where he remained during the rest of the war. When the allies arrived, they captured Willigut in his home. He then suffered from a stroke, possibly caused by shock, which left him paralyzed and unable to speak. He moved back to Germany, even though his health was poor. Karl-Maria Willigut-Weisthor died on January 3, 1946 in Arolsen. (Private Collection)

Himmler and Karl Wolff at the Wewelsburg castle. (MIHAG-CH)

Himmler with his Adjutant Hajo von Hadlen and Karl Wolff. (Author's Archive)

Photo taken in early 1939. This was the last time Himmler visited Wewelsburg before the war. (Private Collection)

Himmler and Heydrich leave Wewelsburg after a visit. (Private Collection)

Luftwaffe General Ludwig Wolff, Heinrich Himmler, Karl Wolff and Rudolf Querner. Rudolf Querner enlisted in the army in 1912. After the war broke out he was taken prisoner of war in 1914 and was not released until 1918. He joined the police in 1919 and served with the Germanderie until 1935. Querner then went to the Schutzpolizei. During the occupation of Czechoslovakia in 1939, he led an Einsatzgruppe in Bohemia. Querner served as HSSPF of "Nordsee," "Donau" and Mitte" areas during the war. He committed suicide on May 27, 1945. (Mark C. Yerger)

Opposite: Himmler shakes hands with Dr. Bernhard Frank. At left, Manfred von Knobelsdorf. Dr. Bernhard Frank belonged to Himmler's staff. He was later to be the last commander of SS-Wachtbatallion "Obersalzberg," the SS guards at Hitler's mountain residence. The guard battalion at Obersalzberg was heavily expanded during the war. Eventually, more than 3000 SS guards served there. (Author's Archive)

Himmler, Karl Wolff, Anton Vogler and Friedrich Karl Freiherr von Eberstein. Note the different issues of collar tabs. Von Eberstein was the man who introduced Reinhard Heydrich to Himmler. He held the post as HSSPF for SS-Oberabschnitte "Süd" and "Main," the only person to have been in command of two main SS Districts at the same time. Anton Vogler was born on September 5, 1882. He served in the First World War as an artillery officer and won the Iron Cross for bravery in combat. He joined the SA in 1933, the SS in 1935 and held a post as instructor at the SS-Junkerschule "Tölz" until 1936. After some time as an instructor at SS-Junkerschule "Braunschweig," Vogler was transferred to SS-Oberabschnitt "Süd." He held various posts but mainly as a staff officer. He was the deputy for von Eberstein as HSSPF "Süd" and commander of SS-Oberabschnitt "Süd" in 1945. (Mark C. Yerger)

A photo with many of the highest leaders of the SS and the state. From left to right are Arthur Seyss-Inquart, Reichsleiter Martin Bormann, Dr. Ernst Kaltenbrunner (successor to Heydrich as commander of the RSHA), Hitler, Himmler, Karl Wolff and Reinhard Heydrich. Both Kaltenbrunner and Seyss-Inquart were born in Austria. They both served in the illegal Austrian NS-Party and prepared for the future Anschluss with Germany. (Author's Archive)

Himmler, Karl Wolff, an NSDAP diplomat and Himmler's driver Lucas. Far right is the shoulder of Jochen Peiper. (Patrick Agte)

Left to right are Wilhelm Frick, unknown, Joachim Von Ribbentrop and Himmler who enjoys a cigar. The photo was taken in Berlin in 1940. Note that von Ribbentrop wears the Iron Cross won during the First World War. (Private Collection)

Hitler and Himmler with the latest model of a new Porsche. Next to Hitler is Dr. Ferdinand Porsche. He also created the Volkswagen, a project for the German people. It meant that everyone should be able to buy their own car, but few cars were delivered when the production was changed in prepare for the war. The classic Volkswagen "Beetle" is one of the most manufactured cars ever. (Author's Archive)

Himmler with soldiers of the Wehrmacht and the SS. Karl Wolff is shown in the background. (Jürgen Weiner)

Himmler, Karl Wolff and Joachim von Ribbentrop. Von Ribbentrop was viewed as a "career" Nazi who was always striving to please Hitler. He went to Canada as a young man and worked building bridges. Like most foreigners in Canada, he dreamed of being successful and having money. His family owned banks and was influential in the arena of politics. Von Ribbentrop returned to Germany in 1914 and participated in the First World War. He married the daughter of a champagne producer and was the owner of the famous brand name of "Henkel-Trocken." His father-in-law brought him into the company to learn the wine business. Influenced by Hitler, he joined the NSDAP in 1932. Hitler often visited von Ribbentrop's and it was in his house that Hitler formed his first cabinet. When Hitler assumed power in Germany, he made an independent department for von Ribbentrop, called "Dienststelle Ribbentrop," where he was authorized to undertake special foreign assignments. Hitler sent him on a disarmament tour in Europe where he succeeded in forming a British-German naval agreement in June of 1935. Hitler was more than satisfied with his accomplishments and, in August 1936, von Ribbentrop was appointed ambassador to Great Britain. The English were very upset when he saluted the King of England with the Hitler salute. In 1938, von Ribbentrop formed the Rome-Berlin Axis, that later would include Japan. Hitler made him Minister of Foreign Affairs in February of 1938. In August of 1939, von Ribbentrop was sent to Moscow to work out the details regarding the future of Poland which Hitler and Stalin had agreed upon. Von Ribbentrop and the Russian Foreign Minister, Molotov signed the famous non-aggression pact also called "The Molotov-Ribbentrop Pact." In this pact Germany and Russia agreed not to attack each other, a pact Hitler later broke when he launched Operation Barbarossa in 1941. With this pact Poland's fate was sealed. Von Ribbentrop held his post as minister until May 1945. He was arrested by the British in June 1945 and was prosecuted in the Nürnberg trial. Found guilty on all counts, he was sentenced to death by hanging. He was the first to be executed on October 16, 1946. His last words were "God protect Germany." (Author's Archive)

Himmler and, in glasses, Gauleiter Dr. Alfred Meyer. Meyer participated in the First World War as Oberleutnant and was taken POW by the French. Meyer was not released from prison until 1920. He came back to Germany and found in Hitler's "Mein Kampf" what he had searched for. He joined the NSDAP in 1926 and worked for a time as a miner but began to study economics. With Gauleiter Florian of Düsseldorf he fought the communists in the Ruhr area. He was appointed Gauleiter for Westfalen-Nord with seat in Münster in 1931 and remained at this post until 1945. During 1941 Meyer was appointed Staatssekretar and Deputy Reichsminister of the occupied "Ostgebite," Ostministerium under Alfred Rosenberg. Meyer represented Alfred Rosenberg at the Wannsee conference in January 20, 1942. He was awarded the War Merit Cross with Swords First and Second classes. Holder of the Golden NSDAP Party badge, he was also awarded the NSDAP service badge in silver. To avoid being captured, Dr. Alfred Meyer committed suicide near the river Weser in April 1945. (Private Collection)

Himmler inspects an archeological excavation of a graveyard in 1937. Many such excavations were made over the years. There was even a project to find the holy chalice that Jesus drank out of during his last meal. Himmler supported several such expeditions but mostly with poor results. The full truth about the progresses in those excavations will probably never be revealed. (A. Althoff)

Himmler talks to one of the many workers at the Wewelsburg. The Obersturmführer on Himmler's right is unidentified. (A.Althoff)

From left to right are Himmler, Dr. Ernst-Robert Grawitz, unknown SS-Untersturmführer and Hanns Johst. Grawitz participated in the First World War and was awarded the Iron Cross second class and Ehrenkreuz für Frontkämpfer. He joined the SS in 1933 and received the rank of SS-Sturmbannführer. Grawitz served as commander of the doctors in the SS with the title Reichsarzt-SS. (Author's Archive)

Himmler and Mattihas Kleinheisterkamp pay a visit to the 6.SS-Division "Nord." Kleinheisterkamp had a varied career in the SS. He participated in the First World War and then joined the Freikorps. He joined the SS in 1933 and rose quickly in rank. After serving as an instructor at
the SS-Junkerschule "Braunschweig," he became Chief of Staff to Paul Hausser and the SS-VT in 1936. He resigned from this post in 1938 after
a quarrel with "Sepp" Dietrich. Kleinheisterkamp served as a battalion commander in the "Das Reich" Division and was awarded both classes
of the Iron Cross during the Polish campaign. He was then transferred to the "Totenkopf" Division as a regimental commander. He briefly led
the division when the commander Theodor Eicke was wounded, before Georg Keppler succeeded him. Kleinheisterkamp was then assigned to
command the "Das Reich" Division in 1942 and at that command won the Knight's Cross. When the future SS division "Nord" was formed,
Kleinheisterkamp was appointed commander. He fought in Finland with "Nord" and was awarded the Finnish Cross of Freedom, 1st class. He
deputized for Felix Steiner as commander of the III.(Germanische)SS-Panzer-Korps in 1944. His last command was of the XI.SS-Panzer-
Korps, fighting in the Küstrin area. He was taken prisoner on April 29, 1945, and committed suicide the next week. On May 9, 1945,
Kleinheisterkamp was posthumously awarded the Oakleaves to his Knight's Cross. (MIHAG-CH)

Himmler and Matthias Kleinheisterkamp inspecting soldiers of the SS-Division "Nord," which Kleinheisterkamp commanded between April 20, 1942, and December 15, 1943. (Mark C. Yerger)

Himmler during a visit to SS-Division "Das Reich." From left are Walter Krüger, Himmler, Paul Hausser and Jakob Fick. (Mark C. Yerger)

A photo from the visit to "Das Reich." Walter Krüger (center) was born in 1890. He participated in the First World War and won both classes of the Iron Cross. He first joined the SA and came to the SS in 1934. During the war Krüger commanded the SS-Polizei-Division as well as "Das Reich." In 1944 he was assigned to command the VI. Waffen-Armee-Korps, that contained the Latvian SS divisions. He held this position until the war ended. Krüger committed suicide on May 20, 1945, on the Baltic front. (Mark C. Yerger)

Himmler reviews SS-Regiment "Germania" in 1940. The officer next to him is regimental commander Karl-Maria Demelhuber who had participated in the First World War. Demelhuber won both classes of the Iron Cross, the German Cross in Silver and the rare Finnish Freedom Cross, 1st class. (Marc Rikmenspoel)

Himmler inspecting tanks on the eastern front. (Marc Rikmenspoel)

Himmler pays a visit to Klagenfurt in 1941. He was visiting SS volunteers who were training there. (H.T Nielsen Collection, MIHAG-DK)

Himmler greets soldiers of the schwere (Heavy) SS-Panzer-Abteilung 502. (Author's Archive)

Himmler and Wilhelm Bittrich arrive at the Castle Elverdinge, Belgium on April 4, 1943. At that time the future 9. SS-Panzer-Division "Hohenstaufen" was being formed. The man on the stairs greeting Himmler is SS-Sturmbannführer Baldur Keller, then General staff officer of the "Hohenstaufen" Division. In October 1944, Keller was transferred to the staff of II.SS-Panzer-Korps as First General Staff Officer. He then served once more under Bittrich, who was the Korps commander. (MIHAG-CH)

Himmler walks the stairs into the castle in Elverdinge. At the top of the stairs regimental commander Ernst Deutsch greets him. Deutsch transferred to the SS-Gebirgs-Jäger Regiment 13 "Prinz Eugen" as regiment commander. He was awarded the German Cross in Gold for bravery in combat. (MIHAG-CH)

From left to right are an unknown SS-Hauptsturmführer, Himmler and Wilhelm Bittrich. The photo was taken on April 4, 1943, in the park of the castle in Elverdinge, Belgium. Wilhelm Bittrich replaced Thomas Müller as commander of the formation staff. Bittrich then led the division until June 29, 1944, when Thomas Müller replaced him. Bittrich's new assignment was to lead the II.SS-Panzer-Korps. (MIHAG-CH)

At the cemetery in Armentieres in the spring of 1943 are Himmler, Wilhelm Bittrich and SS-Obersturmführer Ernst Heindl. Behind Heindl, almost invisible, is SS-Obersturmbannführer Ernst Deutsch, commander of SS-Panzer-Grenadier-Regiment 19 "Hohenstaufen." Heindl served at this time as Deutsch's regimental adjutant. He began his career as an officer in the "Der Führer" Regiment of the "Das Reich" Division. He was then attached to the 3rd battalion of SS-Infantry Regiment 11. Heindl returned to the "Der Führer" Regiment as regimental adjutant before his transfer to "Hohenstaufen." He held this post until August 1944, when he became the commander of the 7th company of SS-Panzer-Grenadier-Regiment 10 "Westland", SS-Panzer-Division "Wiking." In November of 1944, Heindl succeeded Walter Schmidt as commander of the 2nd Battalion of SS-Panzer-Grenadier-Regiment 10 and held that post until the end of the war. (MIHAG-CH)

Dr. Josef Goebbels talks to Himmler. On Himmler's left stands Kurt Daluege, chief of the Ordnungspolizei and later SS-Oberstgruppenführer. Next to Goebbels stands Admiral Wilhelm Canaris, chief of the Abwehr, the counterintelligence of the High Command of the armed forces. Canaris participated in the First World War as a navy officer. During 1915 and 1916 he carried out secret missions for the German navy in Spain. He remained as a naval officer after the war and in 1935 took charge of the Abwehr. In this position he was a rival to Reinhard Heydrich, commander of the SD. The SD also made efforts in the counterintelligence area. Canaris and Heydrich were good friends since Heydrich's days as naval officer in the beginning of 1930s. He was an often-seen guest in the home of Canaris, both he and his wife enjoyed Heydrich's performances on the violin. As the war continued, Canaris began to distance himself from National Socialism. A peaceful man who hated violence, he was soon in the circle of those who planned to murder Hitler. Together with Army General Ludwig Beck, Canaris organized resistance cells. He still kept his contact with Heydrich but after Heydrich was assassinated in 1942 he had no person in Himmler's inner circle. Canaris was one of those who conspired against Hitler that ended in the attempt to kill him on July 20, 1944. Before this happened, Canaris was dismissed from his post as head of the Abwehr in February 1942. The Abwehr was later absorbed by Heydrich's SD, now under SS-Obergruppenführer Dr. Ernst Kaltenbrunner. Canaris was arrested for his part of the plot and was sent to Flossenburg concentration camp. There he was executed by hanging on April 9, 1945. (Author's Archive)

The following documents were written by SS-Oberstgruppenführer Kurt Daluege and contain details of the funeral of Reinhard Heydrich. The document pertains to the ceremony in Prague prior to Heydrich's body being sent back to Germany. The official state funeral was held in the mosaic hall of the Reich Chancellery. (Author's Archive)

The translation of Kurt Daluege's notes are as follows

Timed program for the funeral ceremony in memory of SS-Obergruppenführer Reinhard Heydrich, Sunday June 7, 1942.

07.45 Transferring of the coffin from Reinhard Heydrich Hall to the catafalque followed by the honor guard.

08.00 Admittance of the German and Czech civilian population to the courtyard for last respects. Laying of flower bouquets and wreaths.

14.00 The honor guard is relieved by 8 SS officers, all close associates of Heydrich.

16.00 The honor guard is relieved by the appointed 1 SS-Obergruppenführer, 2 SS-Gruppenführer.

17.00 The courtyard is closed to all. The space in front of the courtyard is sealed off.

17.   The invited guests may enter the courtyard.

17.40   The funeral parade is to stand in company formation in the following order. The musician corps and the music corps of the Leibstandarte. Then one battalion from the Waffen-SS, the "Leibstandarte" with the banner of "Leibstandarte" in front of the column. Then followed by one company of the airforce and the army, one company of the labor service and one company of the order police.

17.45 The formation of the participants in the funeral ceremony is complete.

17.48 President Dr. Hacha arrives.

17.50 SS-Gruppenführer Streckenbach and Nebe, two Generals of the Wehrmacht (Army and Airforce), two leading personalities of the Party (NSDAP), and two SS-Brigadeführer of the Waffen-SS shall replace the honor guard at the coffin. The carriers of the pillow with Heydrich's medals and distinctions shall stand in front of the coffin.

17.55 Heydrich's family members and relatives arrive. The following are to participate: The children Klaus and Heider, Heydrich's mother, Heydrich's brother and sister, Heydrich's father in law, Heydrich's wife's cousin, and one uncle and aunt to Heydrich.

17.59 The Reichsführer-SS arrives in front of the castle. The funeral ceremony is to be supervised by SS-Gruppenführer Krüger.

18.00 The Reichsführer-SS stands at his designated place in front of the coffin. The funeral ceremony begins. Music: AS-Major sonata by Beethoven, played by the music corps of the Order Police.

18.15 Speech given by SS-Oberstgruppenführer Kurt Daluege

18.35 The music corps plays the SS Loyalty song.

18.40 A non-scripted speech is given by the Reichsführer-SS followed by the laying down of wreaths. The children of Heydrich lay down flower bouquets, during which the artillery battery fires its salute. Other wreaths are placed on both sides of the coffin by SS-Oberstgruppenführer Daluege and State Secretary (Karl-Hermann) Frank, followed by wreaths from the Reichssicherheitshauptamt, Army, Airforce, and from the Government of the Protectorate.

18.50 National Songs.

18.55 After the completion of the songs, the carriers lift the coffin. The coffin is carried through the middle path to the waiting gun carriage located in front of the honor gate. The coffin is then loaded on to it. The Reichsführer-SS and the family and the honor group that belongs to the funeral ceremony follow the coffin to the carriage. During the time when the coffin is carried from the catafalque to the carriage the honor guard is saluting with a military salute. At the same time the parade march is played. The march ends when the Reichsführer-SS lowers down his arm that has been raised to salute. The musician corps and the music corps of the Order Police shall as soon as possible take their places at the courtyard. For the funeral march, they'll line up in front of the right gate of the courtyard. Holding their wreaths, the wreath bearers form into marching formation at a designated location in the courtyard. The carrier of the pillow (displaying Heydrich's awards) joins the wreath carriers in marching formation. During the funeral march the different carrier groups will keep a distance of 30 meters between each other and from the first and last units of the march.

19.05 The commander of the funeral parade gives the order to start the funeral march. The participating formations are placed so they can march by the coffin in mourning march-beat. The formed funeral march at right consists of the musician corps, the music corps of the Order Police and the wreath carrier company who will fall-in in front of the honor company of the Order Police. On the order of SS-Gruppenführer Krüger, the musician corps and the music corps of the Order Police commence the mourning march throughout the review. The order is not given in formation during the funeral march.

19.25 The mourning march is to form behind the carriage in the following order: The first row is to contain SS-Oberstgruppenführer Daluege, SS-Gruppenführer Frank, Heinz Heydrich and Mrs. Heydrich's cousin Mr. Wiepert. Five meters to the rear, the second row contains the highest participating SS officers, and five meters behind this grouping should march the other honor guests in order of rank.

20.40 The funeral march arrives at the train station. The honor formations stop on the right side of the road, faces left and salutes the gun carriage containing the coffin of Heydrich. On order of the company commander the formation follows the coffin with their eyes.

20.45 While the musician corps and the music corps of the Waffen-SS play the parade march, the coffin is transferred from the gun carriage. The coffin is carried into the train station followed by the funeral march and wreaths.

20.50 The coffin is loaded on to the awaiting train. Honor and following formations are to take their places as soon as possible. All attendees and guests in the train station are to salute the departing train during which time the song "Ich hat einen Kameraden" (I had a comrade) is played by the SS music corps.

Signed
Daluege
SS-Oberstgruppenführer and
Colonel-General of the Police

Berlin 6 June 1942

████████████rg ██-█r. 1o8o 6.6.1942 15.o5 – EB –

Minutenprogramm für die Trauerfeierlichkeiten für
SS-Obergruppenführer H e y d r i c h am Sonntag,dem 7.Juni 1942.-

---

7.45 Uhr   Überführung des Sarges aus der Reinhard Heydrich-Halle
           der Burg auf den Katafalk,begleitet durch die
           Ehrenwache.-

8.oo Uhr   Einlaß der deutschen - und Tschechischen Bevölkerung
           zur letzten Ehrung in den Burghof.Niederlegung von.
           Blumensträußen und Kränzen.

14.oo Uhr Ablösung der Ehrenwache durch 8 SS-Führern die engsten
           Mitarbeiter von Heydrich.-

16.oo Uhr Ablösung der Ehrenwache durch die bestimmten
           1. SS-Obergruppenführer und 2.SS-Gruppenführer.-

17.oo Uhr Der Burghof wird für die Bevölkerung geschlossen.Der
           Vorplatz vor dem Burghof,der Burgstätterring,wird
           abgesperrt.-

17.██ Uhr Die geladenen Gäste können den Burghof betreten.-

17.4o Uhr Die ████████e steht in Kompaniefront in folgender.
           Rei█████████ntereinander:
           Spielmannszug und Musikzug der Leibstandarte-
           1 Bataillon Waffen-SS Leibstandarte Adolf Hitler mit
           Fahne der Leibstandarte- 1 █████ █ ███ffe -
           1 Kompanie Heer- 1 ██████ █ ███ █ ██ Kompanie-
           stärke- 1 Kompanie ████ ███ ███ .-

17.45 Uhr Die Aufstellung der ███████ ██ ██ ███ ████ ██ ██ ist
           beendet.-

17,48 Uhr Eintreffen des Staatspräsidenten Dr. H a c h a .-

17.5o Uhr Übernahme der Ehrenwache am Sarge durch SS-Gruppenführer
           und Generalleutnante der Polizei Streckenbach und Nebe.-
           ████████le der Wehrmacht (Heerund Luftwaffe) 2 Führende
           ████████ der Partei- 2 SS-Brigadeführer und
           ███████ der Waffen-SS.Die Ordenskissenträger mit den
           ████████ichnungen von Heydrich vor dem Sarg.-

17.55 Uhr   Eintreffen der Familienangehörigen und der Verwandten
von Heydrich.- Es nehmen teil:-
Die Kinder Klaus und Heider,-die Mutter von Heydrich,-
der Bruder und die Schwester von Heydrich,-der Water
von Frau Heydrich,- der Vetter von Frau Heydrich,-
ein Onkel und eine Tante von Heydrich.----

17.59 Uhr   Der Reichsführer -SS trifft vor der Burg ein.Die
Trauerparade wird von SS-Gruppenführer K r ü g e r
gemeldet.---

18.00 Uhr   Der Reichsführer -SS steht auf seinem Platz vor dem
Sarge.-Die Trauerfeier beginnt.--
Musikstück : AS-DUR-Sonate von Beethoven,gespielt
von einem Musikkorps der Ordnungspolizei.---

18.15 Uhr   Rede von SS-Oberst-Gruppenführer D a l u e g e .--

18.35 Uhr   Die Musik spielt das SS-Treuelied.--

18.4o Uhr   Gedenkworte des Reichsführers-SS und Niederlegung des
Kranzes.Niederlegung der Blumensträusse durch die
Kinder Heydrichs,während der Niederlegung des Kranzes
schießt die Batterie Salut.Weitere Kranzniederlegungen
rechts und links vom Sarg durch SS-Oberst-Gruppenführer
Daluege,Staatssekretär Frank,Kränze des
Reichssicherheitshauptamtes,des Heeres,der Luftwaffe,
der Protektoratsregier... .---

18.5o Uhr   Nationalhymnen.--

18.55 Uhr   Nach Beendigung der Nat... ... ... Sarg-
träger an den Sarg und ... ... -Der Sarg
wird durch den Mittelga... ... ...rtor
aufgefahrenen Lafette getragen und dort befestigt.-Es
folgen dem Sarge bis vor die Lafette"Der Reichsführer-",
die Familienangehörigen und führende Ehrengefolge,das
den Trauerzug begleitet.Während des Tragens des Sarges
von dem Katafolk zur Lafette erweist die angetretene
Trauerparade die Militärische Ehrenbezeugungm unter
... des Präsentiermarsches.- Der Präsentiermarsch
...gebrochen,wenn der Reichsführer -SS seinen zum
...erhobenen Arm senkt.Auf dem Burghof selbst
...t sich der Spielmannszug und der Musikzug der
...lizei schnellstens zum Trauermarsch vor dem
...tor zum Burghof.

Zu	18.55 Uhr	Die Kranzträger mehnen die Kränze auf und formieren ihren Marschblock auf dem vorgeschriebenen Platz im Burghof.-Die Polizei-Standarte setzt sich hinter die Kapelle der Ordnungspolizei auf dem Burghofe.Den Marschblock der Kranzträger beschliessen die Träger mit Kranz des Reichsführers-SS und die Träger der Ordenskissen Heydrichs.Beim Trauermarsch selbst haben diese Trägergruppen untereinander und von den vor ihnen marschierenden oder folgenden Teilen des Trauerzuges 3o Meter Abstand zu nehmen.---
	19.o5 Uhr	Der Führer der Trauerparade gibt den Befehl zum Abmarsch des Trauerzuges.Die angetretenen Formationen sind so aufgestellt,dass sie am dem Sarge im Trauermarschritt vorbeimarschieren.Die am rechten Burgtor aufgestellten Trauerzugformationen,bestehend aus Spielmannszug und Musikzug Ordnungspolizei, . Kranzträgerkompanie,gliedern sich vor der Ehrenkompanie der Ordnungspolizei in den Trauerzug ein.Der Spielmannszug und Musikzug der Ordnungspolizei spielt auf Befehl des SS-Gruppenführers Krüger zum Vorbeimarsch der Formationen vor der Lafette,den Trauermarsch,der auch nicht beim Eingliedern in den Trauerzug unterbrochen wird.---
	19.25 Uhr	Das Trauergefolge schlie ... ... mit dem Sarg an in folgender Erste Reiche -SS-Oberst-... ... SS-Gruppenführer Frank,- ... ... Vetter von Frau Heydrich,-Herr W i e p e r t .---- Im Abstand von 5 Metern folgt in Sechserreihen das anwesende höchste SS-Führerkorps.Diesem SS-Führerblock folgen in 5 Meter Abstand die übrigen Ehrengäste,ihrem Dienstrange entsprechend.--
	2o.4o Uhr	Ankunft der Trauerparade am Bahnhof.Die Ehrenformationen halten an der rechten Strassenseite,machen links um und grüssen zum letzten Male die vorfahrende Lafette mit dem Sarg von Heydrich.Auf Befehl des Kompanieführers die Augen folgen dem Sarge.-- ... wird von der Lafette genommen unter Spiel des

Blatt 4

Zu	20.45 Uhr	<u>des</u> Präsentiermarsches durch den Spielmannszug und Musikzug der Waffen-SS,solange bis der Sarg in den Bahnhof hineingetragen ist.Trauergefolge und Kränze folgen.--
	20.50 Uhr	Der Sarg wird im Sonderzug verladen.- Ehren-und Begleitkommandos nehmen schnellstens ihre Plätze ein.Die Trauergäste,die noch den Bahnhof betreten haben,grüssen den Zug bei seiner Abfahrt unter Spiel des Musikzuges SS,"Ich hatt`einen Kameraden.--"

gez.- D a l u e g e

SS-Oberst-Gruppenführer und
Generaloberst der Polizei.--

Berlin,den 6.Juni 1942

F. d. R.

SS-Hauptsturmführer

Himmler holds hands with the children of Reinhard Heydrich. (Author's Archive)

Himmler with the children of Reinhard Heydrich in Prague 1942. They are standing watching the funeral procession of the murdered Heydrich. His remains were taken back to Germany where he received a state funeral. (Author's Archive)

The coffin with Heydrich's remains is at the podium in the mosaic hall at the Reich Chancellery. The guard of honor belongs to the SD. (Author's Archive)

Hitler gave the speech of honor for Heydrich at his funeral. Heydrich's funeral was performed in the mosaic hall of the new Reich Chancellery. The coffin was brought back from Prague with great ceremony. In Prague there was a monument built with a bust of Heydrich. The Czechs destroyed the monument after the war. (Author's Archive)

Himmler salutes the grave of Reinhard Heydrich. (LB)

SS men guard the memorial bust of Heydrich in Prague. (Author's Archive)

Himmler visits the 7. SS-Freiwilligen-Gebirgs-Division "Prinz Eugen." From left to right are Himmler and Karl Wolff. Far right is the divisional commander Arthur Phleps. Phleps fought in three different armies before Russian soldiers killed him on September 21, 1944. He was born into the Austrian-Hungarian Empire in 1881 and fought for the monarchy in the First World War. The Treaty of St. Germain put his home under the Romanian flag. Phleps came into the Romanian army and formed the mountain troops. He rose to the rank of General but after a quarrel with the army command resigned. In 1940 he managed to go to Berlin and was accepted into the Waffen-SS. First serving with the divisional staff of the SS-Division "Wiking," he was next assigned command of SS-Regiment "Westland." In 1942 he was reassigned to form a new mountain troop of the Waffen-SS, the eventual SS-Division "Prinz Eugen." Soldiers from outside the Reich formed more than 85 % of the Division and the division fought with success in Yugoslavia. In September 1944, Phleps took command of the front sector in his homeland of Siebenburgen. Soon after, he accidentally crossed into Soviet-held territory while on a reconnaissance mission and was captured. Luckily for Phleps the Russians didn't know who he was or what position he held. Ironically, the result of a German air-attack killed Phleps and his men. The Russians shot them all to prevent their escape. His son, also a Waffen-SS soldier, received the posthumously awarded Oakleaves that his father was to wear. Years later, Phleps' daughter sought out the remains of her father. She found them and now he rests in a grave with his men and Russian soldiers. (Marc Rikmenspoel)

Himmler inspects the soldiers and their equipment of the Prinz Eugen Division. (Private Collection)

Himmler with Phleps again. On Himmler's right stands Karl Wolff speaking to an unidentified SS-Standartenführer. (Private Collection)

Himmler pays a visit to the "Prinz Eugen" Division in 1943. From left are Heinz Johst, Karl Wolff, an unknown SS-Standartenführer, the divisional commander Arthur Phleps, the HSSPF for Serbia August Edler von Meyszner and then Himmler. Meyszner was born in Austria and participated in the First World War. He joined the illegal Austrian SA and was imprisoned for his political activities. Meyszner escaped to Germany after his release and joined the police force in Berlin. He then held various posts in the SS and ended the war as inspector of the Gendarmerie and Schutzpolizei. After the war he was tried for war crimes in Belgrade for his time as HSSPF there. He was found guilty and was hanged on January 24, 1947. (Private Collection)

Himmler visits the 6th SS-Division "Nord" in summer of 1942. From right to left are Himmler, Hans-Georg Goebel, unknown and H. Rahn. (Marc Rikmenspoel)

Himmler visits Waffen-SS troops in 1942. (Neill Thomson archive)

Himmler greets an SS skier from the SS-Schiibatallion during a competition. According to his sleeve band, he is attached to SS-Oberabschnitt "Mitte," located in Braunschweig. (Jürgen Weiner)

Himmler with SS cavalry soldiers in July 1941. (Mark C. Yerger)

Himmler, Karl Wolff and the SS-Obergruppenführer Heinrich Schmauser inspecting soldiers of the 34th SS-Fuss-Standarte in December 1934. This SS unit was based in Munich and was popularly called "Oberbayern." This photo was taken in Weilheim and the unit was formed in September of 1930. (Author's Archive)

Himmler is visiting Waffen-SS troops on his birthday, October 7, 1944. (Mark C. Yerger)

This photo was taken in the autumn of 1940. Himmler is visiting the 3rd company of SS-Ersatz-Bataillon "Der Führer." (Patrick Agte)

Himmler watches the destruction of a railway with an army general. Probably taken in Russia. (Author's Archive)

Himmler inspects SS recruits. (Patrick Agte)

Himmler salutes soldiers of the 16th company of the "Deutschland" Regiment. They have had a marching exercise with full armor pack. This unit was led by Otto Weidinger, later a Swords holder and last commander of the "Der Führer" Regiment of the "Das Reich" Division. The photo was taken in 1938 in Hamburg. (Marc Rikmenspoel)

Right: Himmler as usual, being surrounded by SS officers. (A.Althoff)

Below: A smiling Himmler with Gauleiter Hugo Jury and Dr. Max Thomas of the SD. (Marc Rikmenspoel)

Right: Hitler, Himmler, Paul Hausser and Karl-Maria Demelhuber during a field inspection. (Marc Rikmenspoel)

Below: Left to Right: Karl Gebhardt, Fritz Ehrath, Himmler and, in the background, Walter Krüger. Karl Gebhardt was a doctor who later became the head surgeon of the SS. He was convicted in the Nürnberg "Doctors" trail for illegal medical experiments and was hanged on June 2, 1948. (Marc Rikmenspoel)

Himmler congratulates Alois Weber for receiving the German Cross in Gold. Weber would later also be awarded the Knights Cross. He served with the Deutschland Regiment of the SS-Division "Das Reich." Weber was awarded the Knight's Cross on June 30, 1943, as an SS-Hauptscharführer while in hospital for wounds. He would later become an officer, ending the war as SS-Untersturmführer. (Marc Rikmenspoel)

Himmler speaks to an Army General. (Private Collection)

Himmler practices shooting while SS officers observe. The officer next to Himmler is probably "Sepp" Kiermeier. (Author's Archive)

Above, Opposite: Himmler on a picnic with officers from his personal staff. Second from right stands Karl Wolff. (A.Althoff)

Below, Opposite: Himmler's visit to Grodno at the eastern front. The photo was taken on June 30, 1941. Himmler studies a map while Karl Wolff watches. (Private Collection)

Himmler on one of his inspection trips. (Private Archive)

Himmler lights a cigar. The man on right is probably his driver Bastian. (Private Collection)

Photo of Himmler while visiting troops in the field. Himmler talks with a Wehrmacht officer. (Author's Archive)

Himmler inspects early SS-VT troops. One of Röhm's dreams was to replace the old army with the SA, a notion Hitler refused. There were, however, SS troops who were trained like the regular army. These troops would later become the Waffen-SS, which at its peak totaled over 900,000 soldiers. These troops were considered the elite forces of Germany and the requirements for joining were strict. They were highly respected, even by the troops they fought against. (Mark C. Yerger)

Stuttgarter Jllustrierte

STADT DER AUSLANDSDEUTSCHEN
Nr. 52   30. Dezember 1942   20 Pfg.

Frei Haus 22 Pfg. Ausland mit ermäß. Porto 30 Pfg., Italien 2 Lire, Frankreich 4 frs., Schweiz 40 Rappen, Spanien Ptas. 1.25, Portugal 2 Esc., Ungarn Filler -.36, Belgien 2 bfrs., Holland 20 Cents, Bulgarien 8 Lewa, Rumänien 12 Lei, Schweden 48 Öre.

Der Reichsführer ⚡⚡ bei den Volksdeutschen in der Süd-Ukraine

Heinrich Himmler, der Reichsführer ⚡⚡ und Chef der deutschen Polizei, überbrachte den Volksdeutschen in dem Gebiet der Süd-Ukraine die Grüße des Führers. — Das Sieg-Heil auf den Führer am Schluß einer Kundgebung, an der auch die volksdeutsche Jugend begeistert teilnahm.

Heinrich Himmler, Comandante dell'arma ⚡⚡, ha portato il saluto del Führer ai tedeschi dell'Ucraina meridionale.

PK-Aufnahme: ⚡⚡-Kriegsberichter Alber

Stuttgarter Jllustrierte

STADT DER AUSLANDSDEUTSCHEN
Nr. 41   13. Oktober 1943   20 Pfg.

Frei Haus 22 Pfg. Ausland mit ermäß. Porto 30 Pfg., Italien 2 Lire, Frankreich 4 frs.,
Schweiz 40 Rappen, Spanien Ptas. 1.25, Portugal 2 Esc., UngarnFiller -.36, Belgien
2 bfrs., Holland 20 Cents, Bulgarien 8 Lewa, Rumänien 20 Lei, Schweden 0.50 Kr.

**Der Reichsführer ⚡⚡ bei den estnischen
Freiwilligen**

Auf einem Truppenübungsplatz im Osten besichtigt der Reichsführer ⚡⚡,
Reichsminister des Innern, Heinrich Himmler, der am 7. Oktober 43 Jahre
alt wurde, Einheiten der estnischen ⚡⚡-Freiwilligen-Brigade und unterhält
sich mit einem Unterführer.   PK-Aufnahme: ⚡⚡-Kriegsberichter Hofstätter (Atl.(

Il Reichsführer ⚡⚡ e Ministro degli Interni del Reich, Heinrich Himmler, che il 7 ottobre ha compi-
ito 43 anni, visita al fronte orientale unità di volontari estoni ⚡⚡ e s'intrattiene con un sottuficiale.

Page 156: Cover from the German magazine "Stuttgarter Illustrated." This magazine was published weekly in several countries in Europe. Himmler is shown in the southern Ukraine visiting the ethnic Germans who lived there. Note that Himmler wears his Golden Hitlerjugend member badge. The man who took the photo is probably Kurt Alber who first served in the SD-Hauptamt. He became an SS-Hauptsturmführer in the Allgemeine-SS and was later transferred to the Waffen-SS as a war correspondent. He was later to serve with the SS divisions "Nordland" and "Götz von Berlichingen" as a war correspondent. Note in the right corner the various prices for the magazine in different European countries. (Christian Habisohn)

Page 157: Cover from the magazine "Stuttgarter Illustrated" from 1943. Himmler visits the Estonian volunteer division of the Waffen-SS. Right behind Himmler stands Werner Grothmann. Far left is Franz Augsberger, divisional commander of the Estonian Division. Augsberger was born in Vienna on October 10, 1905. He left Austria for Germany and joined the SA in 1930 and then the SS in 1932. He was to hold several different posts within the SS. When the Estonian Freiwillige-Brigade was formed, Augsberger was appointed commander. This unit later reached divisional strength. He ended as SS-Brigadeführer and won the German Cross in Gold and the Knight's Cross. Franz Augsberger was killed in action on March 19, 1945 in Silesia. (Christian Habisohn)

From right are: Karl Götz, the councilor of Stuttgart, Hermann Harm, Johannes Johst, Karl Wolff, Himmler, Hans-Adolf Prützmann, Ludolf von Alvensleben and Dr. Hermann Behrends. The other three persons are unknown. They watch a review of ethnic German youths, probably in the Ukraine during 1942. (Christian Habisohn)

Photo of Himmler, Hans-Adolf Prützmann, Himmler's adjutant Werner Grothmann and Karl Wolff. Himmler talks to the ethnic German doctor, Dr. Johann Classen, the head of a hospital in Halbstadt. (Christian Habisohn)

Karl Wolff, Erich von dem Bach and Himmler are shown from left to right in this photo. It was taken during an inspection trip to Russia in 1941. (LB)

Himmler is having a conversation with a prisoner of war. (Author's Archive)

Above, Opposite: Himmler visiting a Soviet POW Camp during the war. In the background is Erich von dem Bach who served as a HSSPF in Russia. (Author's Archive)

Below, Opposite: Himmler, with SS-Obergruppenführer Werner Lorenz, talks to ethnic Germans in Poland during 1939. (Author's Archive)

Himmler (left) visits Russia and talks to a Russian youth. In center is the Higher SS and Police leader for Russland-Mitte, Erich von dem Bach. Almost covered on the left is Karl Wolff. (LB)

Karl Wolff, Himmler and an unidentified police officer. The photo was taken in Russia where Himmler speaks with a Russian boy. (Author's Archive)

Above, Opposite: Hermann Fegelein, Karl Wolff, Himmler and Erich von dem Bach in Russia during 1941. Hermann Fegelein was to be one of Himmler's closest subordinates. He was the commander of the Waffen-SS Cavalry Division "Florian Geyer" and won the Swords to the Knight's Cross. At the end of the war he held the post of Himmler's personal liaison officer at Hitler's HQ. (Mark C. Yerger)

A photo that was taken in Russia shows Himmler on a round trip in the occupied parts of the country. In this photo the Reichsführer-SS inspects a farming village. (LB)

Himmler talks to a captured Russian political officer. Behind Himmler are Karl Wolff and Himmler's bodyguard "Sepp" Kiermeier. On the left stands the HSSPF for "Russland-Mitte," Erich von dem Bach. (A.Althoff)

Above, Opposite: Himmler inspects female SS members. There were several Female SS members and most served as nurses in field hospitals. (LB)

Below, Opposite: A time of fun. Karl Wolff, Himmler and an unknown person seem to share a joke. (A.Althoff)

This photo was probably taken during a field inspection. To Himmler's left is Karl Wolff. (A.Althoff)

Himmler, Franz Ziereis and Dr. Ernst Kaltenbrunner in the summer of 1942. Kaltenbrunner succeeded Reinhard Heydrich after his murder as commander of the RSHA (Reichsicherheitshauptamt). After the war Kaltenbrunner was prosecuted in the Nürnberg trial and was sentenced to death. He was hanged in 1946. (Mark C. Yerger)

Himmler watches a field parade of "Totenkopf" cavalry soldiers. The man behind Himmler in steel helmet is Hermann Fegelein, later commander of the cavalry division "Florian Geyer." When he married Eva Braun's sister, Gretl, it was Himmler who performed the wedding ceremony. The wedding was carried out at Hitler's house in Berchtesgaden, the Berghof. Even though Fegelein and Hitler were related by marriage, it did not save Fegelein's life in 1945. (Mark C. Yerger)

Himmler visiting the 13th SS-Division "Handschar" which contained Bosnian soldiers. The photo was taken in October 1943 at Neuhammer, Silesia. (A.Althoff)

Himmler converses with SS soldiers of Hitler's Begleitskommando (Escort commando). Behind Himmler walks SS-Standartenführer Hans Rattenhuber and the man Himmler is shaking hands with is Erich Kempka, Hitler's chauffeur. (Author's Archive)

Himmler takes a rest from his inspection of the "Das Reich" Division. Far left is Walter Krüger and next to Himmler, Karl Gebhardt. (Marc Rikmenspoel)

Right: Mattihas Kleinheisterkamp, Himmler and XVIII.Gebirgs-Korps commander Franz Böhme. This photo was taken in 1942 during Himmler's visit to the SS-Division "Nord." (Marc Rikmenspoel)

A photo taken in the Netherlands at the school for the SS and SD in Auegoor during February 1944. Front row from left to right are van Geelkeren, Dr. Arthur Seyss-Inquart, Himmler, Anton Mussert, Hanns-Albin Rauter, Karl-Maria Demelhuber and Erich Naumann. (Mark C. Yerger)

A Photographic Chronicle of Hitler's Reichsführer-SS

Above, Opposite: Photo from one of the Waffen-SS schools in the Netherlands. Far left stands Carl-Maria Demelhuber, whose command oversaw the schools. Third from left is Hanns-Albin Rauter, then Himmler. The soldiers are using the rapid MG-42 machinegun. Hanns-Albin Rauter held various posts in the SS. He served on Himmler's personal staff and also in the SS-Hauptamt. Rauter also served as Stabsführer in the SS-Oberabschnitt "Südost" before receiving the post of Höhere SS und Polizeiführer "Nordwest." This post included occupied Holland and he was also the leader of SS-Oberabschnitt "Nordwest", the name for the occupied Holland. Rauter was captured after the war and tried for war crimes. He was found guilty and was hanged on March 25, 1949. (Marc Rikmenspoel)

Below, Opposite: Hitler leads the way to the Kroll Opera for a Reichstag meeting on May 4, 1941. Behind Hitler are Karl Wolff and Himmler. (Patrick Agte)

Right: Wilhelm Keitel, Karl Dönitz and Himmler listen while Hitler is giving a speech. Karl Dönitz, the successor to Hitler, started his career in the German navy. He participated in the First World War and was assigned to the ship "Breslau." He fought in the Near East with the Turks against the Russians in the Black Sea. In 1916, Dönitz was transferred to the U-boat fleet and served as commander of U-boat U68. In the last days of the war a torpedo hit Dönitz' U-boat and it was sunk. He was taken prisoner of war by the British and was incarcerated until July 1919. When he returned to Germany he was appointed inspector of the U-boat fleet and stationed at the Naval headquarter in Berlin. Dönitz was a devoted Nazi and one of the few high ranking Navy officers to join the NSDAP. Hitler gave him the awesome responsibility of reconstructing Germanys new U-boat fleet. Dönitz was convinced that the U-boat fleet would be one of the most important elements of the German war machine. Unlike Raeder, he thought that the heavy battleships were easy targets that could not maneuver effectively under fire. Dönitz completely reformed the U-boat fleet but was not comfortable with its size when war broke out. He wanted more time to increase the size of the fleet and to hone its combat skills. He was appointed commander of the U-boat fleet on September 12, 1939. His "Wolf Pack," as they were called, was deadly

effective after the war started. Dönitz introduced the strategy of the mass attack by his U-boats, which was responsible for sinking several hundred thousand tons of allied shipping. The convoys could not adequately defend themselves against such a strategy. After the battles in the West, Dönitz was able to provide his U-boats with the necessary access to Atlantic Ocean. Gigantic U-boat bunkers were built on the coast of France that could withstand a direct hit from any type of air attack. From these bases in France, the U-boats could operate over the entire Atlantic Ocean. In the beginning, their method of operating met with little resistance until British sonar was introduced. Along with this was the capture of the German code machine "Enigma" which was taken from a damaged U-boat. The British were then able to break the German code and from that point the Allies could read every message that was sent. On January 30, 1943, Dönitz was appointed successor to Erich Raeder as commander of the German navy. The next day,

Dönitz was appointed Gross-Admiral and he led the German navy until May 1945. His fanatical belief in Hitler and victory for Germany resulted in many casualties as the navy received orders to fight to the last man. In the final days of the war Dönitz was appointed to succeed Hitler as Führer and leader of Germany. After Hitler's suicide, he formed his government at the old navy school in Flensburg where he tried to negotiate with the allied forces. He decided to send several ships to the Baltic in order to rescue fleeing German soldiers and civilians from the Russians. This, his last major plan, was a success and tens of thousands of German citizens were rescued. Dönitz stood trial in Nürnberg for war crimes. He was sentenced to ten years in prison and sat in the Landsberg prison until October 1, 1956. He kept close contact with his former naval officers and lived a peaceful life in retirement near Hamburg. Karl Dönitz died on December 24, 1980. (Author's Archive)

From left to right are Himmler, Wilhelm Keitel, Walther von Brauschnitz and Erich Raeder. Erich Raeder graduated from the navy cadet school and was commissioned an officer before the First World War. For a time he was assigned to the private yacht of the Emperor Wilhelm II. When the war started, Raeder took part in various operations involving the coast of England. He remained in the navy after the war and in 1928 became head of the Naval Command. He impressed Hitler with his advocacy for heavy battle ships as the backbone of a new German fleet. These were called the "pocket" battleships. He was not a devoted Nazi and joined the NSDAP late. He did, however, accept the award of the Golden NSDAP member badge in 1937. In 1935, Raeder was appointed commander of the German navy. He held that post until 1943 when Hitler ordered him to retire. He was promoted to Gross-Admiral in 1939. Raeder was the man behind the invasion plans for Norway in 1940, as he understood all too well the importance of access to the Atlantic Ocean. His influence with Hitler diminished as the war progressed and Karl Dönitz replaced him in 1943. Raeder was accused of war crimes in the famous Nürnberg trial and was sentenced to life imprisonment in 1946. He was released on September 26, 1955, due to bad health. Erich Raeder died on November 6, 1960 in Kiel Germany. (Author's Archive)

Hitler, Hermann Göring, Wilhelm Keitel, Karl Dönitz and Himmler at a parade in 1943. At this point in time many of the high leaders had realized that Göring should never be the successor to Hitler. When Hitler committed suicide in 1945, his post went to Gross-Admiral Karl Dönitz, the commander of the German Navy. Wilhelm Keitel was born on September 22, 1882. He participated in the First World War as an officer and won the Iron Cross. After the war he was attached to the army and for some time to the Minister of Defense. Keitel was made commander of the OKW (High Command of the Armed Forces) after the affair with Werner von Blomberg and Werner von Fritsch. In 1938 Keitel was promoted to General but had no real powers despite his title. He was a tool for Hitler and performed his orders without ques-tions. After the successful battle in France he was made General Field Marshal in July 1940. Keitel did not agree with Hitler's plans to at-tack Russia and wanted to resign from his post. He succumbed to pres-sure from Hitler and remained in his position. His influence decreased during the war due to opposition to Hitler's plans and formation moves. Keitel remained at Hitler's side until the end. He was prosecuted in the Nürnberg trial and was sentenced to death for war crimes. Even though some orders that had been given were against his will, he fol-lowed orders himself. Keitel fought in court for saving the life of Alfred Jodl who according to Keitel had had subordinate position. He asked to be shot instead of hanged. Both attempts were in vain and Wilhelm Keitel was hanged in Nürnberg on October 16, 1946. (Author's Archive)

Right: This photo depicts one of the most important moments of Himmler's career. He has just been appointed Minister of Interior, a post that Wilhelm Frick held before him. Himmler was appointed Minister of Interior on August 25, 1943. This moment was probably the apex of his career. Himmler would have this post until April 29, 1945, when Hitler expelled him from the NSDAP and all his assignments within the Reich. This was due to Himmler's attempts to negotiate a separate peace treaty with the Western Allies so that the German forces could concentrate all their remaining resources on the eastern front. (LB)

Below: Himmler as "Reichs Commissar für die Festigung des Deutsche Volksturms," is shown looking at types of houses that were to be built in the occupied territory. The photo was taken in March of 1941. On the right is Rudolf Hess who later that year flew to England on his famous peace mission. The man in civilian clothes to Himmler's right is Fritz Todt, Minister of Armaments and Ammunition. Fritz Todt was born on September 4, 1891, in Pforzheim. His father was a famous owner of a jewelry plant. He attended the Gymnasium and after his graduation went to Munich and studied technology at a collage between 1911 and 1914. When the First World War broke out, Todt enlisted in the service and served on the Western front as an officer. In 1916 he became a flying observer and was badly wounded in an air battle. After the war he attended a technology course in Karlsruhe from which he graduated in 1920. He joined the NSDAP in 1922 and his civilian profession was a technical engineer of construction. He joined the SA and SS in 1931 and held a place in the SA-High command. In July of 1933, Todt became the commander of the new German highway system called the Autobahn. Under his command the highways were expanded to cover most of Germany. He was also appointed leader of the Organization "Todt," named after him and served with the so-called "Four Year Plan" under Hermann Göring. He was involved in several major construction projects such as the West Wall fortresses. In 1940 Todt was appointed Minister of Armaments and Ammunition, being responsible for the construction of weapons and war products. He held this position until 1942. After leaving a meeting with Hitler at his headquarters in Rastenburg, his airplane crashed on February 8, 1942. There are several theories concerning his death, since he was a skilled pilot and was also a General-Major of the Luftwaffe. It is known that he disagreed with Hitler on several points regarding the construction of weapons and war products. If his death was a suicide or if foul play was involved no one really knows. Albert Speer replaced him and commanded the Organization "Todt" until 1945. (LB)

Himmler speaks to Max Faust, the construction manager of the I.G Farben company. The photo was probably taken in 1942 during Himmler's inspection trip to the I.G Farben plant in Auschwitz. (Jürgen Weiner)

Below: Himmler inspects models of planned houses to be built in occupied territories for German immigrants. On his right stands Rudolf Hess and on his right Martin Bormann in SS uniform. In the background on the left is Jochen Peiper. Rudolf Hess, the deputy Führer of the Third Reich is widely known for his flight to Scotland in 1941 in an attempt to negotiate with the British for a separate peace. Hess was one of the first members of the NSDAP and was a former soldier of the First World War. He served first in the infantry but was later transferred to the air force. Hess followed Hitler in every step he took and served as Hitler's personal secretary. He participated in the putsch of 1923 but was never convicted for his role. He went to prison on his own initiative with Hitler. Hess was to write major parts of the first volume of Hitler's Mein Kampf that Hitler dictated to him. When the NSDAP was rebuilt in 1925, Hess stood in the immediate inner circle around Hitler and had his own staff of co-workers to follow Hitler's orders. One of his young staff members was Martin Bormann who soon made himself invaluable to Hess. When Hess flew to Scotland it was Bormann who resumed Hess' duties. Historians have discussed for decades Hess' mysterious flight to Scotland but Hess took the truth with him when he died. He was taken prisoner of war in 1941 and was prosecuted for crimes in the major trial that took place. Hess was sentenced to life imprisonment and was put in the Spandau prison with the other convicted prisoners. After all the others were released, Hess remained alone in Spandau and was the only prisoner until he died in 1987. There were several attempts made to release him for humanitarian reasons. The British government refused any such thought. When Hess died rumors started that he had been killed or had committed suicide. The myth of Rudolf Hess continues. (Author's Archive)

Left: Himmler and the chief of the Reichs Chancellery, Hans Lammers. (Private Collection)

Himmler talks with medical doctors. To serve as a medical doctor in Germany without problems, they joined the SS. Of all the professions, none had as many SS members as the medical profession. (Neill Thomson archive)

Above, Opposite: Hitler and Himmler are inspecting the SS-Regiment "Deutschland" in 1938. On the left is SS-Oberführer Paul Hausser and between Hitler and Himmler, SS-Gruppenführer Karl Wolff. (Private Collection)

Below, Opposite: Himmler is representing the Waffen-SS when the commanders of the armed forces congratulate Hitler on his birthday on April 20, 1944. Left to right: Wilhelm Keitel (Wehrmacht), Karl Dönitz (Kriegsmarine) Himmler and Erhard Milch representing the Luftwaffe in Göring's place. (Author's Archive)

Himmler with binoculars and Hugo Eichhorn with Herbert Otto Gille. Eichhorn enlisted in the army and was an officer candidate. Shortly after the war broke out he was transferred to the SS-Pionier Batallion of the "Totenkopf" Division. After graduating from SS-Junkerschule "Tölz," Eichhorn came to SS-Pionier Batallion 5, "Wiking." He distinguished himself during battles near Stalingrad and was seriously wounded in 1943. After his recovery, he was appointed commander of the SS-Pionier-Ausbildungs und Ersatzregiemnt in Dresden. He held that post for the rest of the war. (Marc Rikmenspoel)

Himmler is watching troops from the 5.SS-Panzer-Division "Wiking." On his left stands August Dieckmann who posthumously won the Swords to the Knight's Cross. (Mark C. Yerger)

A scene from Himmler's visit to the SS-Panzer-Division "Wiking." Felix Steiner was awarded the Swords to his Knight's Cross. He was very well liked by his soldiers and was demanding of his officers. He ordered that every one of his officers should without hesitation recognize 50 soldiers of their unit by name. Steiner himself never forgot a face or name. His skills as commander are well documented and his divisional command was the first multi-national division, the later SS-Division "Wiking." Steiner understood how to combine the many different nationalities and their significant skills. He later led the III.(Germanische)SS-Panzer-Korps that commanded three larger multi-national SS-Divisions including "Nordland" and "Nederland." Steiner kept close contact with his friends after the war. He was found dead in his apartment in Munich on May 12, 1966, after suffering a heart attack. (Mark C. Yerger)

Above: Himmler on a visit to the SS-Panzer-Division "Wiking." In the background is divisional commander Felix Steiner. (Mark C. Yerger)

Above, Opposite: From left are: Vidkun Quisling, Himmler, the Reichskommisar for Norway Josef Terboven, the army commander of Norway Nikolaus von Falkenhorst and the Höhere SS und Polizeiführer Wilhelm Rediess. Nikolaus von Falkenhorst was born on January 17, 1885. Joining the army in 1903 he participated in the First World War. During the 1939 Polish Campaign, von Falkenhorst led the XXI Army.

This unit served directly under the command of the OKW during the invasion of Denmark and Norway in 1940 and later parts of it would become the Army High Command for Norway. Von Falkenhorst saw action in Russia during the winter of 1941 and 1942, then returned to Norway. He was appointed Supreme Commander of the Army in Norway and held this post until December 18, 1944, when he was replaced after some disagreements with Reichskommisar Josef Terboven. Von Falkenhorst was tried for war crimes by a British court and sentenced to death. The court later changed the sentence to 20 years imprisonment. Nikolaus von Falkenhorst was released on July 13, 1957, and died on June 16, 1968. (Anders Skötte Collection)

Himmler in Oslo, Norway giving a speech to Norwegian SS volunteers. The year was probably 1942. (Tommy Natedal)

Himmler inspecting the new SS-Standarte "Nordland" in Oslo on February 9, 1941. Norway was occupied on April 9, 1940, and several thousand Norwegians enlisted in the Waffen-SS. Many Swedes made their way to Oslo where the recruiting office was located, when it was forbidden to open foreign recruiting offices in Sweden. The Swedish police had problems keeping the border closed. Many of the Swedish volunteers had served in the Finnish war against Russia and wanted to continue their fight against the communists. (Steve Tashik)

Heinrich Himmler with the National Socialist leader in Norway, Vidkun Quisling. After the German occupation of Norway in 1940, Quisling was made Minister-President. He was only a figurehead while the true leader in Norway was Reich Commissioner Josef Terboven, who in 1945 committed suicide together with the HSSPF for Norway, Wilhelm Rediess. Quisling was prosecuted for high treason after the war, sentenced to death, and executed in 1945. (Author's Archive)

Himmler talks to Norwegian volunteer Arne Hassel, who served in the "Wiking" Division. The photo was taken in Graz, Austria. The Norwegian SS volunteer Thoralv Gjölberg is at right. (Tommy Natedal)

Himmler prepares for giving a speech to the Norwegian volunteers in Miatu during 1943. (Tommy Natedal)

Mitau, Latvia, 1943. Himmler visits the DNL and Jonas Lie is in the background. (Tommy Natedal)

Himmler visits "Den Norske Legion" (Norwegian Legion) on March 16, 1943, in Mitau, Latvia. The SS soldier at far left with Norwegian collar tabs is Rolf Wirum, who later served in SS-Panzer-Grenadier-Regiment 23 "Norge." (Tommy Natedal)

Mitau, March 16, 1943. Himmler watches the Norwegian Legion. (Tommy Natedal)

Himmler inspects the entire "Legion Norwegen" in Mitau on March 16, 1943. From left to right are an unknown SS-Rottenführer, SS-Obergruppenführer Gottlob Berger, commander of the SS-Hauptamt, Himmler, SS-Obersturmführer Olaf Lindvig, Karl Holter, SS-Obersturmführer Erich-Friedrich Dahm, SS-Hauptsturmführer Finn Finson, and at far right, SS-Untersturmführer Meino Dirks. Dahm served as commander of the Ersatz-Batallion of Legion Norwegen. He first served as commander of the 5th Company of Infanterie-Regiment 4. After his assignment in the Ersatz-Batallion, Dahm was transferred to the SS-Division "Nordland" where he later served as commander of the 5th Company of SS-Panzer-Grenadier-Regiment 23 "Norge." (Tommy Natedal)

Left to right: unknown, Himmler, Jonas Lie, unknown. This photo also comes from Himmler's visit to the DNL in Mitau. (Tommy Natedal)

Mitau, 1943. Left to right: Finn Finson, later commander of I. SS-Panzer-Grenadier-Regiment 23 "Norge," unknown, unknown, Himmler, Hans G. Holter (brother of Karl Holter) and Rolf Wirum. (Tommy Natedal)

Mitau, 1943. Himmler inspects an SS-Ersatz-Batallion. In the background stands Jonas Lie as an SS-Sturmbannführer. (Tommy Natedal)

From left to right are Jonas Lie, Himmler, unknown SS-Officer, Karl Holter and an unknown SS-Obersturmführer from Himmler's staff. The photo was taken during the inspection of the DNL in Mitau on March 16, 1943. Karl Holter was a Norwegian poet and a leading member of the Legion's propaganda company. (Tommy Natedal)

(Above, Opposite) Left to right: Himmler, two unidentified SS soldiers, Erich von dem Bach, and probably Friedrich Jeckeln. The man bending over the table is the Norwegian Olaf W. Fermann. The photo was taken in a Russian kindergarten, probably in 1943. Von dem Bach and Jeckeln both served as Höhere SS und Polizeiführer in Russia. Friedrich Jeckeln held several posts during his career in the SS. He began in one of the many SS-Standarten and worked his way up. He led different SS-Abschnitte then SS-Oberabschnitte and served temporarily as police commander in Braunschweig. When Russia was invaded, Jeckeln was appointed HSSPF for the area "Russland-Süd." He later traded his area with Hans-Adolf Prützmann and became HSSPF "Russland-Nord." Jeckeln led several Kampfgruppen during his time as HSSPF. Mostly, these were mixed units of soldiers including regular troops, members of the police force and foreign or local volunteers. He was awarded the Knight's Cross for actions against Russian partisans. He also won the Oakleaves to his Knight's Cross as commander of the V. SS-Freiwilligen-Gebirgs-Korps. He held titular command as HSSPF "Belgien-Nordfrankreich," but a deputy took care of the duties. While in Russia he was placed in Riga, Latvia, and was responsible for several massacres during this time. He was captured after the war and sent to Riga where he stood trial. He was found guilty of war crimes and hanged in Riga on February 3, 1946, one day after his 51st birthday. (Geir Brenden)

(Below, Opposite:) Left to right: Himmler, Gottlob Berger, unknown SS-Officer and Karl Holter. Gottlob Berger was the commander of the SS-Hauptamt and was responsible for the recruiting of soldiers for the Waffen-SS. His office contained several sub-departments for recruiting from foreign nations. (Tommy Natedal)

SS-Hauptsturmführer Jonas Lie. Lie was a Norwegian volunteer and served in the 1st Battalion of the "LSSAH" as an ordinance officer. He was then attached to the Freiwilligen Legion "Norwegen." He reached the rank of SS-Oberführer while serving in the SS-Hauptamt. In the end he went back to Norway and served as police commander. He committed suicide in 1945 to avoid being captured. (Tommy Natedal)

Right: Himmler greets Jonas Lie of the Norwegian Legion. (Author's Archive)

Above, Opposite: February 20, 1944, in Hitler's headquarters in Rastenburg. Left to right: Léon Degrelle, Herbert Otto Gille, Hitler, Hermann Fegelein, Heinrich Himmler and press chief Otto Dietrich. This day Gille was awarded the Swords to his Knight's Cross and Degrelle his Knight's Cross. Himmler often participated in award ceremonies like this. Hermann Fegelein had been assigned as Himmler's liaison officer at Hitler's headquarters on January 1st the same year. In June of 1944 Fegelein married Eva Braun's sister Gretl. (Marc Rikmenspoel)

Himmler talks to Swedish volunteers of the Waffen-SS. Far right, only part of his chest seen, is Walter Nilsson, then Karl-Olof Holm, an Estonian Swede, and the Swedish volunteer X. Karl-Olof Holm served in the Swedish army with Artillery Regiment A8 in the town of Boden. He went to Germany via Finland and served in the SS-Division "Wiking" and was killed in action in October 1944 in Latvia. Nilsson and volunteer X both came from Anti Aircraft Regiment Lv7 in Boden. Nilsson was killed in action on January 25, 1944, near Rogowitzky in Russia. Volunteer X survived the war and lives today as a retiree in Sweden. All three escaped to Finland together and went by the ship "S/S Ockenfels" from Torneo in Finland to Germany. This photo was taken in the training camp "Sennheim." The number of Swedes that served in the Waffen-SS is not known but probably 300-500. There were also Swedes who held positions in the Allgemeine-SS. (Author's Archive)

Herbert-Otto Gille receives the Swords to his Knight's Cross while Himmler observes. (Mark C. Yerger)

Herbert-Otto Gille, Himmler and Léon Degrelle. Gille was the first Waffen-SS soldiers awarded the Diamonds to the Knight's Cross. In this photo he has just been awarded the Swords. Degrelle was a Walloon volunteer who later became the highest decorated non-German when he received the Oakleaves to his Knight's Cross. (Mark C. Yerger)

Léon Degrelle, leader of the Rexist party in Belgium, is giving a speech. Degrelle was a great admirer of Hitler and Germany. He enlisted in the German army and was accepted for duty. He fought at first with the Wehrmacht but was later transferred to the Waffen-SS. Degrelle went to the SS-Division "Wiking" but was soon transferred to the SS-Sturmbrigade "Wallonien." He was a very brave soldier who could encourage his men during difficult times and was awarded the Knights Cross with Oakleaves as well as the German Cross in Gold. This made him the most highly decorated non-German soldier. He was also awarded the Close Combat Clasp in gold for more than 50 days of close combat. Degrelle was wounded several times and received the Wound Badge in Gold. He was in command of the 28. SS-Freiwilligen-Panzer-Grenadier-Division from January 30, 1945, until the war ended. He escaped to Spain in Albert Speer's private airplane. A court in Belgium sentenced him to death in absentia. He lived in Spain and became a Spanish citizen in the middle 1950s. Léon Degrelle died in Spain on April 1, 1994. His last wish to be buried in Belgium was denied by the Belgium government. (Author's Archive)

SS-Brigadeführer Herbert-Otto Gille, later Diamonds to the Knight's Cross holder, Himmler and August Diekmann who later was awarded the Swords. Herbert-Otto Gille succeeded the famous SS-General Felix Steiner as commander of the "Wiking" Division. August Diekmann led SS-Panzer-Grenadier-Regiment 10 "Westland." He was killed in action on October 10, 1943, on the Russian front. Dieckmann was awarded the Swords to his Knight Cross and promoted to SS-Standartenführer posthumously. (Mark C. Yerger)

Left: Himmler inspecting Belgian policemen. The photo was taken in Brussels. (Author's Archive)

Below: Himmler with Anton Mussert, the leader of the National-Socialist Party in Holland. (Author's Archive)

Above, Opposite: Himmler talks to SS-Obergrup-penführer Oswald Pohl, head of the SS-Wirtschaft und Verwaltungshauptamt or SS-WVHA. On Himmler's right stands the NS-Führer of Holland, Anton Mussert. Oswald Pohl was one of the most powerful SS leaders during the Nazi era. He was the head of all concentration camps in and outside of Germany. He also commanded all working projects within the Reich. Pohl was an early member of the NSDAP, joining during 1926. He served as a naval officer and in 1929 joined the SA. Pohl left the Navy and joined the SS on February 2, 1934. He soon became the head of the SS administrative office. He rose quickly in rank and ended the war as an SS-Obergruppenführer. Pohl escaped and hid when the war ended. He was found on a farm working as a laborer. He was sent to prison in Landsberg and tried for war crimes. Found guilty, he was executed by hanging on June 8, 1951. Anton Mussert was an engineer by profession and founder of the National-Socialist Party in Holland. The party was modeled after the German NSDAP organization. When the Netherlands was occupied in 1940, Mussert began to work with the Germans. In 1942 he was appointed leader of the Dutch people. Mussert was arrested on May 7, 1945 and sent to prison. He was tried for high treason and found guilty. Anton Mussert was hanged on May 7, 1946 in The Hague. (Author's Archive)

Below, Opposite: Himmler and Fritz Freitag with the divisional staff of the 14.SS-Division "Galizien." Freitag, shown here as an SS-Brigadeführer, wears his German Cross in Gold. He has not yet been awarded the Knight's Cross. Freitag led the Ukrainian Division through its battles in Russia. He was awarded the Knight's Cross on September 30, 1944, following a recommendation from Himmler. (Mark C. Yerger)

Fritz Freitag, Himmler and the divisional staff of the 14th SS-Division. (MIHAG-CH)

Left: Himmler and SS-Brigadeführer Fritz Freitag inspecting the 14th SS-Division, a division that consisted mainly of Ukrainians who volunteered to fight on the German side. This photo was taken in May 1944 during their training. (Mark C. Yerger)

Above, Opposite: Himmler salutes the Ukrainian volunteers. The man under Himmler is divisional commander Fritz Freitag. (Author's Archive)

Below, Opposite: Himmler and SS-Brigadeführer Dr. Otto Wächter watching a parade in May 1944. Far right stands Fritz Freitag (only his head is visible). (Mark C. Yerger)

Himmler pays a visit to the 14. SS-Division "Galizien" (A. Althoff)

Above, Opposite: Himmler inspects the 14. Waffen-Grenadier-Division der SS "Galizische." On Himmler's left stands Dr. Otto Wächter. On his right is Fritz Freitag. (Mark C. Yerger)

Below, Opposite: Himmler, Fritz Freitag and Dr. Otto Wächter. (Mark C. Yerger)

Himmler visits a volunteer regiment of an SS-Freiwilligen Gebirgs Division. (A.Althoff)

Himmler and Fritz Freitag. Freitag fought in the First World War and was awarded both classes of the Iron Cross. After the war he joined the Freikorps and later the police. When the war broke out he served with a police regiment in Poland. During the war he commanded the 8.SS-Kavallerie-Division "Florian Geyer," the 4.SS-Polizei-Panzergrenadier-Division and the 14.Waffen-Grenadier-Division der SS (Ukrainische Nr.1) composed of Ukrainian volunteers. He won both the German Cross in Gold and the Knights Cross after a direct recommendation by Himmler. He committed suicide on May 20, 1945, when he risked being handed over to the Russians by the British to whom he surrendered earlier on May 8, 1945. (Mark C. Yerger)

(Above, Opposite) Pictured left to right are: Hermann Preiss, Himmler and Otto Baum. Herrman Preiss joined the army in 1919, shortly after the end of World War I. He served with the army until 1934 when he joined the SS-Verfügungstruppe (SS-VT). He served in the artillery detachment of SS-Standarte "Germania" where he was responsible for forming and training the new artillery unit. In 1939, Preiss helped to form the new artillery regiment of the SS-Division "Totenkopf" and later became its commander. He was awarded the Knights Cross on April 28, 1943, as commander of SS-Artillerie Regiment 3 "Totenkopf." Priess was appointed commander for the "Totenkopf" Division when Theodor Eicke was killed. He won the Oakleaves to his Knights Cross on September 9, 1943, and on April 29, 1944, he received the Swords. When "Sepp" Dietrich was appointed commander of the 6. SS-Panzer-Armee, Preiss was given the command of the I. SS-Panzer-Korps. He led the Korps during the fighting in the Ardennes in 1944. In 1945, the I.SS-Panzer-Korps was transferred to Hungary where they fought against the Russians. His Panzer-Korps was pushed back across the border into Austria where he later surrendered. Tried before a court in the so-called "Malmedy" trial, Preiss was sentenced to 20 years in prison. He was released in October 1954 and died on February 2, 1985. (Patrick Agte)

Himmler with Otto Baum in 1943. Baum served with the SS-VT before he was transferred to the "Leibstandarte Adolf Hitler." He was later transferred to the 3.SS-Division "Totenkopf." Between July 28, 1944, and September 23, 1944, Baum was the division commander of "Das Reich." On September 24, 1944, he took command of the 16th SS-Panzer-Grenadier-Division "Reichsführer-SS" which he commanded until the end of the war. He was awarded the Swords to the Knight's Cross and the German Cross in Gold. Otto Baum died on June 18, 1998. Between Himmler and Baum stands "Sepp" Kiermeier, Himmler's bodyguard. (Mark C. Yerger)

Heinz Harmel, Otto Baum, Hitler and Himmler at the award ceremony for Harmel's and Baum's Oakleaves in 1943. Both Harmel and Baum were later awarded the Swords to the Knight's Cross. (Mark C. Yerger)

Hitler awards Karl Ullrich the Oakleaves to the Knight's Cross. Ullrich joined the NSDAP and the SA in 1931. He entered the SS in 1932 and belonged to the 56th SS-Standarte that was based in Bamberg. Ullrich came to the SS-VT and was in the first class of SS-Führerschule in "Braunschweig" in 1935. He served with the "Reich" Division during the battle in the West. Ullrich was transferred to the "Totenkopf" Division in 1941. He commanded the SS-Pionier Batallion 3 and won the Knight's Cross at this position. He later served as a detachment commander, regimental commander and then division commander. He was made temporary commander of the "Totenkopf" Division between June and July 1944. On October 9, 1944, he was given the command of the 5. SS-Panzer-Division "Wiking," at which post he remained for the rest of the war. Note the Demjansk shield on his arm. Karl Ullrich died in May 1996. (Marc Rikmenspoel)

Karl Ullrich receives the Oakleaves to the Knights Cross from Hitler. Himmler seems to avoid the camera. (Mark C. Yerger)

From left to right are Karl Wolff, Himmler, Theodor Eicke and Matthias Kleinheisterkamp. (Marc Rikmenspoel)

Above, Opposite: Kurt Daluege, Benito Mussolini, Heydrich, Himmler and Karl Wolff in Italy in 1938. Kurt Dalegue was born on September 15, 1897, in Kreuzburg and participated in the First World War. When the war was over, Daluege joined one of the many Freikorps in Germany, the Rossbach group. He joined the NSDAP in 1922 but left after the failure of the beer-hall putsch in 1923. He had formed the first SA-Group in Berlin during that time. Daluege joined the party again in 1926 and led SA-Unit "Berlin-Nord." Daluege joined the SS on July 25, 1930, and was attached to the later SS-Oberabschnitt "Spree." When Hitler came to power in 1933, Daluege was climbing high in the new government. His rival, Himmler, tried to eliminate him through Heydrich but failed. Daluege was appointed commander of the Ordnungspolizei (Order Police) in 1936 and held this position until 1943. He was one of four that reached the rank of SS-Oberstgruppenführer and the only one who held this rank within the police. He was in charge of the funeral ceremony of Heydrich in Prague in 1942 and later to succeeded Heydrich as Reichsprotektor of Böhmen-Mähren. He also held this post until the war ended. When the war was over, Daluege was prosecuted for war crimes and tried in court in Prague. He was found guilty and hanged on October 20, 1946. (Author's Archive)

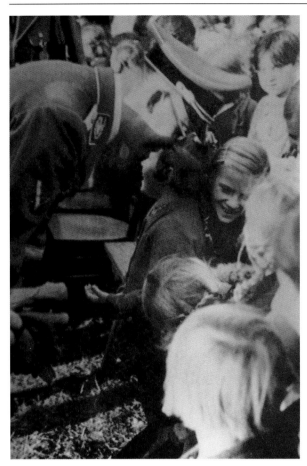

Himmler visits a school in Warthegau in May 1941. (Patrick Agte)

Himmler at a diplomatic meeting in Italy 1938. Left to right: Kurt Daluege (later head of ORPO), the German ambassador Ullrich von Hassel (executed in 1944 for his role in the assassination attempt on Hitler) Karl Wolff and Reinhard Heydrich. (Mark C. Yerger)

Left to Right: Heydrich, Italian Police commander Bocchini and Himmler during a visit to Rome in 1940. (Patrick Agte)

In September 1940 Himmler is visited by the Spanish head of the security police, Count des Maydale. They are walking through the "Leibstandarte" barracks. On Himmler's right the commander for the guard battalion, "Teddy" Wisch. (Patrick Agte)

Above, Opposite: Himmler in Rome in 1938 with, at left, the Police commander in Italy, Arturo Bacchini. Karl Wolff stands between hem. (Patrick Agte)

Below, Opposite: Jochen Peiper watches Himmler and the Spanish General Moscardo am Alkazar during a visit to Spain. (Patrick Agte)

Himmler shakes hands with the security police commander in Spain, Count des Mayalde. (Patrick Agte)

Left: Himmler arrives at Kaiserslauten in 1943 for the formation ceremony of the new SS-Division "Hitlerjugend." (Marc Rikmenspoel)

Above, Opposite: Kaiserslauten 1943. Himmler watches members of the Hitlerjugend marching by. They are celebrating the formation of the SS-Division "Hitlerjugend." (Marc Rikmenspoel)

Below, Opposite: Himmler and the leader of the Hitlerjugend, Arthur Axmann, inspecting the newly raised 12.SS-Panzer-Division "Hitlerjugend" in 1943. Axmann replaced Reichsjugendführer Baldur von Schirach on August 4, 1940. The HJ division was formed from Hitlerjugend members but also veterans from other division, mainly from the "LSSAH." Axmann joined the Hitlerjugend in 1928 and was full of desire for a place in the corps. He also spent some time as a soldier at the Russian front but returned soon to his boys. At the end of the war he fought with a battalion in Berlin and was charged with desertion but it has never been proven. (Mark C. Yerger)

Photo from Kaiserslauten in 1943. Himmler is saluting young boys from the Hitlerjugend. (Marc Rikmenspoel)

Opposite: Himmler in Kaiserslauten during 1943. He is inspecting the formation of the new SS-Division "Hitlerjugend." Next to Himmler walks Reichsjugendführer Arthur Axmann. Just behind Axmann walks Gerhard Hein. Hein started his career in the Wehrmacht where he won the Knight's Cross and later the Oakleaves. He was then transferred to the Hitlerjugend Division and is here seen in the political uniform of the Hitlerjugend. Hein finally received the rank of SS-Sturmbannführer and served as a General Staff officer within the SS-Panzer-Division "Hitlerjugend." (Marc Rikmenspoel)

```
          xxxxxxxx
SS-Ustuf. W i t t m a n n
1.SS-Pz.Div. "LSSAH"                    (A) 4140
           über
Heeresgruppe Süd                        31.1.44


Zur Verleihung des Eichenlaubes sende ich
Ihnen meine herzlichsten Glückwünsche und
Grüße.

                        gez. F. Himmler.

    F. d. R.


      (Kment)
SS-Sturmbannführer und
V.O.d.NF-SS b. OKH /PA
Tgb.Nr. 120/44
```

A congratulation note from Himmler to SS-Untersturmführer Michael Wittmann on the occasion of the award of the Oakleaves to the Knights Cross. Wittmann was the most successful Panzer commander of the German armed forces. His reputation was widely known even to his opponents. His first tank kill occurred in early 1943 and he was to receive the Knights Cross, the Oakleaves and the Swords before the end of 1944. Winning this combination of Knights Cross, Oakleaves and Swords within a year is unique and gives a clue to the remarkable performance of Wittmann and his crew. He refused to receive the Knights Cross until his gunner, Bobby Woll, also received it. Wittmann first served with the heavy 13th company of the SS-Panzer Regiment 1 "LSSAH." This company was later reorganized as the heavy Panzer Detachment 101/501 (s.SS-Pz.Abt. 101/501). (Author's Archive)

Opposite: Kurt "Panzermeyer" Meyer, Max Wünsche, "Sepp" Dietrich, Himmler and Hubert Meyer are shown on January 30, 1944. In this photo Max Wünsche is being promoted to SS-Obersturmbannführer. Wünsche had been adjutant to Hitler in the beginning of the war. He was then adjutant to "Sepp" Dietrich. In the end he was the commander of SS-Panzer-Regiment 12 "Hitlerjugend." Wünsche along with adjutant Georg Isecke and the regimental doctor were captured by the British in Normandy during 1944. (Mark C. Yerger)

```
Der Reichsführer-SS          Feldkommandostelle,den 19.6.1944




Ich befürworte den Vorschlag zur Verleihung des
Eichenlaubes mit Schwertern zum Ritterkreuz des
Eisernen Kreuzes an den
SS - Obersturmführer  W i t t m a n n ,.Michael
Kompanie-Führer  2.(s)SS-Pz.Abtlg. 1o1.


                        gez.  H. H i m m l e r

F.d.R.


SS - Sturmbannführer
```

A commendation note from Himmler regarding the Swords to SS-Obersturmführer Michael Wittmann's Knights Cross. Wittmann received the Swords to his Knights Cross on June 22, 1944. The day before he had been promoted to SS-Hauptsturmführer. Wittmann was awarded this decoration personally from Hitler at his headquarter in Rastenburg. After a few days leave he returned to heavy Panzer Detachment 101 and replaced SS-Sturmbannführer Heinz von Westernhagen as commander. Michael Wittmann was killed in action on August 8, 1944. (Authors Archive)

SS-Untersturmführer Michael Wittmann. This photo was taken when Wittmann had been awarded the Oakleaves to his Knight's Cross. (Jess T. Lukens)

Der Reichsführer-SS
Adjutantur

Tgb.Nr.: 640/44
Gro/Dr.

Feld-Kommandostelle, 22.3.1944

23. MRZ 1944

1.) An das SS-Personalhauptamt, Berlin
2.) An das SS-Führungshauptamt, Berlin

Der Reichsführer-SS hat befohlen:

1.) SS-Standartenführer S t r e c k e n b a c h wird mit sofortiger Wirkung von dem Auftrag der Führung der 8. SS-Kavallerie-Division entbunden und mit der Führung der 19 (lett.) SS-Freiwilligen-Infanterie-Division beauftragt.

2.) SS-Obersturmbannführer R u m o h r wird mit sofortiger Wirkung mit der Führung der 8. SS-Kavallerie-Division beauftragt.

3.) SS-Standartenführer B o c k (bisher Führer der Kampfgruppe 4. SS-Panzer-Grenadier-Division) ist sofort zurückzurufen. Vor weiterem Einsatz, den der Reichsführer-SS sich vorbehält, ist ihm ein vierwöchiger Urlaub zu gewähren.

Ich bitte um entsprechende Veranlassung.

[signature]

SS-Sturmbannführer
und Adjutant RF-SS

A document signed by Himmler's adjutant Werner Grothmann concerning three senior officers. Grothmann, acting on direct orders from Himmler himself, he had full authority to act in Himmler's name.

The Reichsführer-SS orders:

1- SS-Standartenführer Streckenbach will, effective immediately, leave his post as commander of the 8. SS-Kavallerie-Division and assume command of the 19. Lettische SS-Freiwilligen-Infanterie-Division.

2- SS-Obersturmbannführer Rumohr will, effective immediately, take command of the 8. SS-Kavallerie-Division.

3- SS-Standartenführer Bock (now commander of a Kampfgruppe in the 4. SS-Panzer-Grenadier-Division) will immediately be recalled. Before reassignment, the Reichsführer approves a four-week vacation.

Signed

Grothmann
SS-Sturmbannführer
and Adjutant RFSS

(Neill Thomson Archive)

Bruno Streckenbach as an SS-Gruppenführer wearing his Knight's Cross. Streckenbach was born on February 7, 1902 in Hamburg and did not participate in the First World War due to his studies. He joined the army in 1918 but never saw combat. In March of 1919 he joined the Freikorps in Hamburg and later in June the Reichswehr. In 1930, Streckenbach joined the NSDAP and the SA at the same time. In 1931 he left the SA for the SS where he remained until the war ended. Two years later, Streckenbach was selected by Heydrich to serve in the SD where he was responsible for the day to day operation of its personnel department. Like the SS, the SD had divided Germany into several different sections called SD-Oberabschnitte. Streckenbach was the commander of SD-Oberabschnitt Hamburg, later renamed Nordwest. He held this post until September 1939, and, when the war broke out, led an Einsatzgruppe during the war in Poland. In 1939 a new organization was formed, called the RSHA. In 1940, he was appointed commander for Amt I of the RSHA, the department involving personal questions. He was also appointed as the Inspector of the Sipo and SD schools. Streckenbach transferred to the Waffen-SS in 1943 and served in the SS-Kavallerie Division under Hermann Fegelein. In September 1943, when Fegelein was wounded, Streckenbach assumed command of the division. He was ordered to leave "Florian Geyer" Division to command the newly formed Lettische Freiwilligen Division der SS, replacing its first commander, Hinrich Schuldt. Streckenbach was considered an exceptional division commander and was awarded both classes of the Iron Cross, the German Cross in Gold, and the Knight's Cross with Oakleaves. He led the Lettische Division until the war ended. He was captured by the Russians and was held prisoner until 1955 when he returned to Germany. He was arrested twice for war crimes but was released. Streckenbach lived the rest of his life in Hamburg where he died on October 28, 1977. (Author's Archive)

Jochen Rumohr was born in Hamburg on August 6, 1910. He and Bruno Streckenbach had many things in common, both joined the NSDAP and the SA in 1930 and both would later serve as division commander of the SS-Division "Florian Geyer." Like Streckenbach, Rumohr left the SA in 1931 and joined the SS where he served with the 4th SS-Standarte in Hartenholm. He then left the Allgemeine-SS for the SS-Verfügungstruppe, the forerunner to the "Das Reich" Division. He served in the Artillerie Regiment of the SS-VT and participated in the war in Poland as a battery commander. Rumohr came to the Kavallerie Division in 1942 where he commanded the artillery regiment. On March 22, 1944, Himmler's adjutant Werner Grothmann wrote: "SS-Obersturmbannführer Rumohr effective immediately will assume command of the 8. SS-Kavallerie-Division Florian Geyer." He replaced Bruno Streckenbach who left for the Latvian SS-Division. Rumohr led the division with success and was awarded the Oakleaves to his Knight Cross. The "Florian Geyer" Division was engaged in heavy combat in and around Budapest, suffering enormous losses. Rumohr committed suicide on February 11, 1945 when his division's breakout from Budapest failed. (Author's Archive)

Friedrich-Wilhelm Bock was born on May 6, 1897. He joined the army in 1914 and participated in the First World War as an artillery officer. After the war, Bock joined the Schutzpolizei in Hamburg where he remained until 1926. He joined the NSDAP in 1933 and continued his service in the police force where he held various posts. In 1940 he joined the Polizei Division and was assigned to the artillery regiment as commander of the II.Detachment. He fought in Russia with success and was awarded both classes of the Iron Cross and the Knights Cross on March 28, 1943. Bock later became regimental commander of the artillery regiment. Parts of the Polizei Division remained to fight in Russia as an SS battle group that he commanded. Bock also commanded the Lettische Freiwilligen Division der SS for a short time before Bruno Streckenbach replaced him. He later assumed the command of the SS-Panzer Division "Hohenstaufen," temporarily replacing Sylvester Stadler. For his bravery during the battles in Normandy he was awarded the Oakleaves to his Knights Cross. When Stadler returned, Bock served in the II/SS-Panzer-Korps as the Corps Artillery commander, a post he held for the rest of the war. Friedrich-Wilhelm Bock died on March 11, 1978. (Author's Archive)

A photo of Werner Grothmann taken in 1940. Grothmann came to Himmler's staff in 1940 as 2nd adjutant, during the time Jochen Peiper served as 1st adjutant. When Peiper returned to the "LSSAH," Grothmann became 1st adjutant. Later he was appointed chief adjutant to Himmler and held this post until the war ended. He was with Himmler when British soldiers captured them in May 1945. (Patrick Agte)

Himmler arrives in Metz, France in April of 1944. He was there to participate in the ceremony creating the new SS-Division "Götz von Berlichingen." (Marc Rikmenspoel)

Himmler is greeted by one of the division staff officers of the new "Götz von Berlichingen" Division. In the background on the right are Werner Grothmann and Fred Conrad. (Marc Rikmenspoel)

The division staff of the "Götz von Berlichingen" Division introduces themselves. From left are SS-Führer from Metz, Himmler, Werner Grothmann, unidentified SS-officer, Fred Conrad and Hermann Buch. (Marc Rikmenspoel)

Himmler is shown with unidentified SS personnel of the "Götz von Berlichingen" Division. The photo was taken in Thouars, France on April 10, 1944. (Marc Rikmenspoel)

A Wehrmacht General salutes Himmler while leaving the ceremony for the newly formed "Götz von Berlichingen" SS-Division. Just behind him is "Sepp" Dietrich in black Panzer uniform. (Marc Rikmenspoel)

"Sepp" Dietrich, Werner Ostendorf and Himmler after the activation ceremony for the new division "Götz von Berlichingen" in Thouars, France on April 10, 1944. (Mark C. Yerger)

Left to right: unknown, Werner Grothmann, Dr. Ludwig Stumfegger of the Führer-Begleit-Batallion, Josef "Sepp" Kiermeier (Himmler's bodyguard), "Sepp" Dietrich, Fred Conrad, Himmler and Carl Oberg. The photo was taken in France, probably on April 10, 1944, during the formation ceremony of the 17.SS-Division "Götz von Berlichingen." (Marc Rikmenspoel)

Himmler talks with Jakob Fick, Knight's Cross holder from the "Das Reich" division. "Sepp" Dietrich talks with the Higher SS and Police Leader Carl Oberg. "Jopp" Fick joined the SS-VT in 1934 in Ellwangen. He was to spend most of his career in the SS-Division "Das Reich." He first held a post as Zugführer in Regiment "Deutschland." He later to served as an instructor at SS-Junkerschule "Bad Tölz." Leaving "Tölz," Fick was transferred to the SS-Kradschützen-Batallion as commander. His unit was to become I/Schnelles (Fast) SS-Kradschützen-Regiment "Langemark" but the regiment was dissolved, and Fick commanded the I. Batallion as an independent unit. As commander, he was awarded the Knight's Cross on April 23, 1943. He held this post until the next month when the battalion was merged with the SS-Aufklärungs-Abteilung 2 "Das Reich." Fick then commanded this reinforced reconnaissance battalion. When the 17.SS-Panzer-Grenadier-Division "Götz von Berlichingen" was formed, Fick was attached to the Division as commander of SS-Panzer-Grenadier-Regiment 37. He also held a short command of the SS-Panzer-Grenadier-Regiment 38 in April and May 1945. Fick also briefly commanded the Division during a few days in March 1945 after division commander Fritz Klingenberg was killed in action on March 22, 1945. (Mark C. Yerger)

Himmler rests with "Sepp" Dietrich (in black Panzer uniform) and SS-Obergruppenführer Carl Oberg, HSSPF in France. Oberg had participated in the First World War and was decorated with both classes of the Iron Cross. He made his career in the SD (Sicherheitsdienst) and served later in the SS und Polizei court in Munich. He was sentenced to death after the war by the British and handed over to the French who also convicted him to death. He was released in 1962 and returned to Germany where he died in 1965. (Mark C. Yerger)

Himmler, "Sepp" Dietrich and Herbert Schuster from SS-Panzer-Jäger-Abteilung 17, "Götz von Berlichingen." (Marc Rikmenspoel)

Two soldiers of the "Götz von Berlichingen" Division demonstrate the proper way to load a rocket launcher in France during 1944. (Marc Rikmenspoel)

Himmler visits the soldiers of the "Götz von Berlichingen" Division. (Marc Rikmenspoel)

Himmler pays a visit to the soldiers of "Götz von Berlichingen." SS-Untersturmführer Erich Hütt stands at Himmler's left and SS-Untersturmführer Heino Schmidt and Herbert Schuster at his right. (MIHAG-CH)

From left to right are Werner Ostendorff, "Sepp" Kiermeier, Jakob Fick, Herbert Schuster, "Sepp" Dietrich, unknown SS-Untersturmführer and Himmler. Werner Ostendorff, here as an SS-Oberführer, was responsible for the formation and served as the first division commander. He began his career in the air arm of the Reichwehr and joined the SS-VT in 1935. He served as a tactical instructor at SS-Junkerschule "Tölz." Assigned as 1a (General Staff Officer) to Paul Hausser in the SS-Division "Reich," Ostendorff participated in the war with Russia. In this position he was awarded the Knights Cross for personal bravery. He led SS-Kampfgruppe "Reich" which was all that remained of the division between February and June 1942. Ostendorff was then appointed to be Chief of Staff for Paul Hausser when he formed the II/Panzer-Korps. He led "Götz von Berlichingen" between November 1943 and November 1944. Before Ostendorf took command of the rearmed SS-Division "Das Reich," he served as the Chief of Staff for army-group "Oberrhein" that was commanded by Himmler. Werner Ostendorff died in an Austrian hospital on May 4, 1945. (MIHAG-CH)

Hitler and Himmler a few hours after the assassination attempt on July 20, 1944. Göring and Benito Mussolini are visible in the background. Himmler received a free hand to find all the traitors who were behind the plot. The chief of the Gestapo, Heinrich Müller, carried out the major work locating every suspicious or eventual opponent to Hitler. For his service, Müller was awarded the Knight's Cross of the War-Merit Cross with Swords. (Author's Archive)

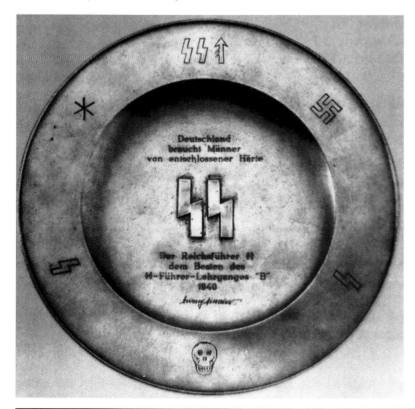

This honor plate is signed by Himmler and awarded to the top graduate officer of SS-Junkerschule "Tölz" in 1940. Both Braunschweig and Tölz had full officer classes that year. (Hermann Historica München via MIHAG-CH)

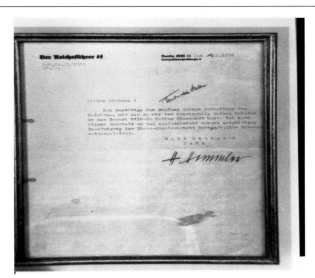

A letter signed by Himmler. (Hermann Historica München via MIHAG-CH)

Der Führer with his "Treue Heinrich" (MIHAG-CH)

Karl Wolff, shown here as an SS-Gruppenführer, was the head of Himmler's personal staff and ended his career as Höchte SS und Polizeiführer for Italy in 1944. Wolff participated in the First World War and reached the rank of Leutnant, winning both classes of the Iron Cross. He joined the NSDAP in 1931 and was attached to the 1.SS-Standarte, which was headquartered in Munich. Later he served as adjutant to Franz Ritter von Epp, the Reichkommisar for Bavaria. Wolff served as Himmler's adjutant between March 1934 and November 1935. He was then appointed to the post of Himmler's chief adjutant and commander of his personal staff. He held various other posts within the SS, which ended with the command in Italy. While in Italy, he was responsible for negotiating for peace with the Allies. Wolff realized that he was taking a risk doing this without prior approval from Berlin. He was severely criticized and was even threatened with the possibility of standing trial for his actions. Wolff would answer and justify his actions only to Hitler in person. He told Hitler about how grave the situation was in Italy and said he had negotiated with the allies only to gain valuable time for Germany. Hitler believed him and cleared Wolff of any and all charges that were pending. After the war he was tried and found guilty for the deportation of Italian Jews. He was imprisoned in 1964 and released in 1971. Karl Wolff passed away on July 17, 1984. (Author's Archive)

Left: A photo of SS-Gruppenführer Karl Gebhardt, Heinrich Himmlers doctor and later head surgeon of the SS. (LB)

Opposite: This document is an SS marriage request submitted by SS-Obersturmführer Sven Rydén, a Swedish SS volunteer. Rydén's bride, Maria Lindström, was born on the island Wormsö in the Estonian archipelago. She and Sven probably met during one of his recruitment trips to Estonia. Sven Rydén was born in Stockholm, Sweden on February 5, 1897. He was one of the oldest Swedes in the Waffen-SS. His career began in the Swedish army but he ran into trouble when he was charged with drunken behavior while in uniform. With the threat of a military court-martial facing him, Rydén fled via Finland to Germany and enlisted for service in the Waffen-SS. Due to his age he was placed in the administrative section and served with the SS-Hauptamt, in Amtsgruppe D II, Germanische Leitstelle. This section was responsible for the recruitment of European volunteers to the SS. Germanische Leitstelle was divided into two sections covering most countries in Europe. Rydén served in the section "Hauptabteilung Nord" that was responsible for the Scandinavian countries, England and Estonia. Such marriage requests were a prerequisite, for no SS soldier was allowed to marry without a formal request stating their background and their family's lineage. Such requests were approved by the Rasse und Siedlungshauptamt who also investigated the backgrounds of the bride. This request is signed by an SS-Brigadeführer of the RuSHA and by Himmler personally. The request was later approved and they were married in 1944. From other records contained in Rydén's SS file, it is mentioned that Rydén and Himmler met personally. (Richard Rydén)

A photo of Himmler during a visit to the front. (Author's Archive)

Sippenakte

Antragsteller: R u b e n , Sven
SS-Dienstgrad: Oftuf.   SS-Nr.:   Sip.-Nr.:   335434

SS-Pflegestelle: Braut/Ehefrau: L i n d s t r ö m , Maria

Abstammung

Gesamturteil: 1: Vermerk!   28.6.1943
Datum

SS-Hauptsturmführer

Erbgesundheit

1. Aufnahme: geeignet/ungeeignet   Datum   Unterschrift und Dienstgrad

2. Heirat:

Der Antragsteller und die zukünftige Braut besitzen die
schwedische Staatsangehörigkeit.

Der Antragsteller wurde in erster Ehe, aus der 2 Kinder
hervorgegangen sind, geschieden. Außer seinen beiden Kin-
dern aus erster Ehe hat der Antragsteller ein unehli-
ches Kind.

In gesundheitlicher und erbgesundheitlicher Hinsicht be-
stehen beim Antragsteller und der zukünftigen Braut keine
wesentlichen Bedenken.

Der Antragsteller ist 46 Jahre, die zukünftige Braut
29 Jahre alt.

28.6.1943
Datum   Unterschrift und Dienstgrad

Vorlage beim
RFSS

Geheim! 1573

Grund: SS-Führer, Antragst. und
Braut schwedische Staatsange-
hörige. Stellungnahme I u.II

Berlin, den 29.6.1943

Der Chef
des RuS-Hauptamtes-SS
i.V.

SS-Brigadeführer

Entscheidung des Reichsführers-SS

Genehmigt	Freigegeben	Freigegeben auf Verantwortung					Abgelehnt Entlassen
		des Antragst.	der zukünftigen Braut	des Antrag- stellers u. d. Braut	der Braut u. b. Antrag- stellers	beider	
	✓						

1. Unterlagen nachreichen

Bemerkungen

Der Reichsführer-SS

Feldkommandostelle, den 30. VI. 43

C/0718. St. & SI

Above, Opposite: Hitler congratulates Himmler on his 44th birthday on October 7, 1944. (Author's Archive)

Below, Opposite: The dead body of Heinrich Himmler. The British, in whose custody he was, took this photo. Himmler with some of his closest men was captured at Bremervorde by a British patrol on May 22, 1945. Himmler called himself Heinrich Hitzinger and hid his identity at first. On May 23 the group was transferred to Camp 031 near Lüneberg. Later that day he made his true identity known. After he was stripped down, there was a small interrogation. He insisted on speaking with General Eisenhower but his wish was ignored. A more careful body search was done after the British found poison in his clothes. The man who examined Himmler's mouth saw something that flashed. Himmler turned his head away and bit a capsule of cyanide. There were several attempts to save his life, but the Reichsführer-SS was dead. Three British soldiers buried him in an unmarked grave in Lüneberg Heide. (Author's Archive)

A rare photo of Swedish SS volunteer, Sven Rydén. Sven Rydén first served in the Swedish army as an Oberleutnant. After being found drunk on duty he risked court martial. He and another Swede, Gunnar Eklöf, fled Sweden via Finland to Germany and enlisted for service in the Waffen-SS. Sven Rydén was 44 years old when he enlisted and because of his age, he was not sent to the front. He came to the SS-Hauptamt and served in the Germanische Leitstelle under Swiss Dr. Franz Riedweg. He worked with the Estonian office and made several radio propaganda speeches for the Estonian population. Rydén was sent to Estonia several times, recruiting volunteers for the Waffen-SS. Himmler asked Rydén to set up a battalion consisting of Swedish Volunteers, named the Freiwilligen-Batallion "Tre Kronor" (Three Crowns). The main idea was to form a Swedish battalion with Swedes, Ethnic Finland-Swedes and Ethnic Estonian-Swedes but the plan was never implemented. The Estonian-Swedes were later transferred to the 20.Waffen-Grenadier-Division der SS (Estnische Nr:1) and to 11.SS-Freiwilligen-Panzer-Grenadier-Division "Nordland." Sven Rydén remained in the SS-Hauptamt until January of 1944 when he was transferred to the RSHA, Amt III B, better known as the SD. Amt III B was responsible for questions regarding Germanic heraldry. On January 20, 1944, Rydén sent a request to the immigration office of the SD, Amt III B4, the office for "Immigration and Resettlement" to immigrate to Germany with his family. According to documents from the Amt III B4, Rydén was accepted as an immigrant and promised a farm in Litzmannstadt, today known as Lodz, Poland, as soon as the war was over. These plans never took place and Sven Rydén was found dead in Berlin on February 19, 1945. He had been shot in the back, probably by another SS man in a quarrel over a girl. The man was arrested and jailed for the murder, but he was never convicted. Due to the chaotic situation that took place during the Battle of Berlin the man was set free and managed to avoid being captured by Russian troops. Sven Rydén was buried in Berlin in 1945. (Erik Rundkvist Archive)

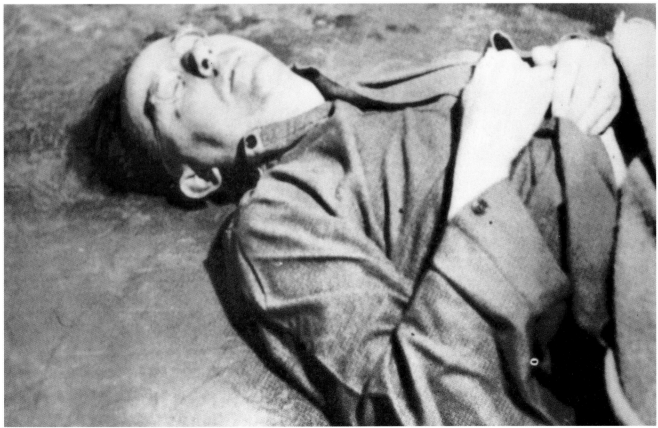

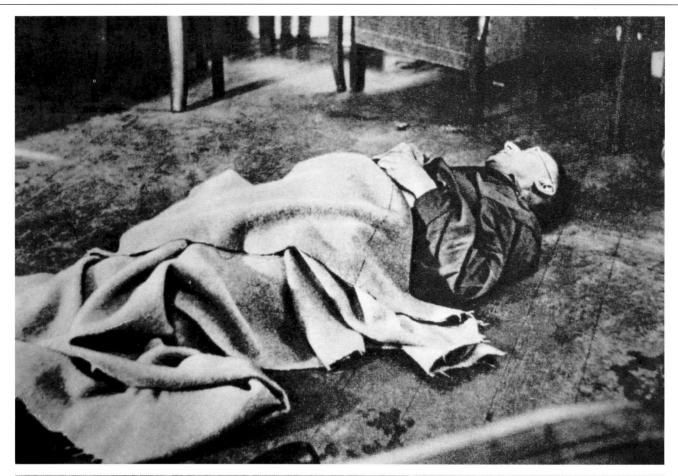

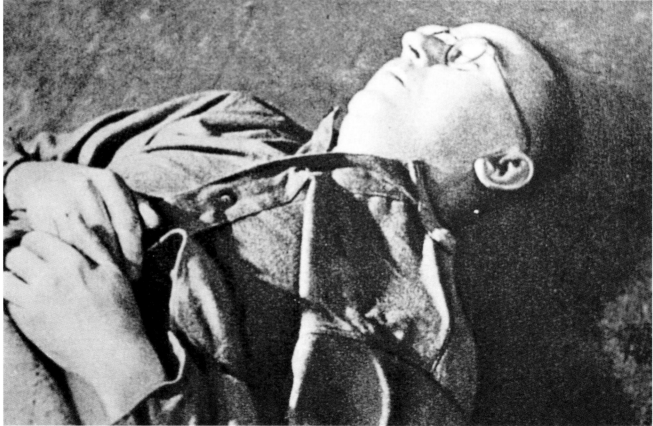

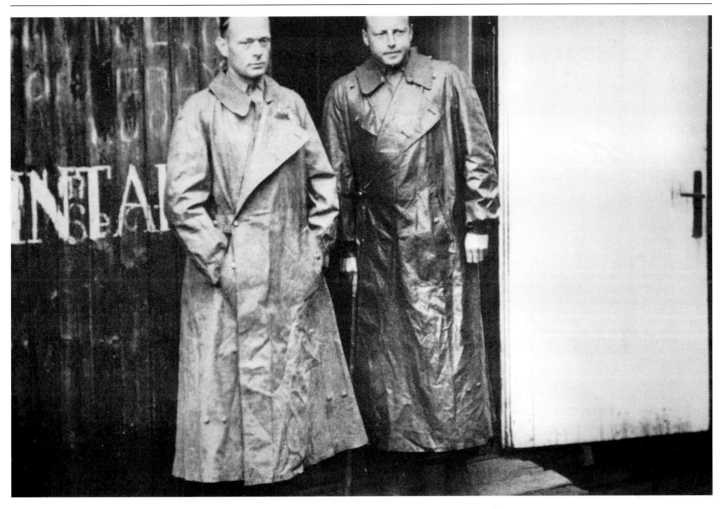

Himmler's adjutant, Werner Grothmann and Heinz Macher. This photo was taken after Himmler's suicide in 1945. Macher was attached to Himmler's staff at this time. British soldiers captured them together with Himmler. Both of them were interrogated and sent to prison. Due to their membership in the SS they were released several years later. (Author's Archive)

Appendix:
Ranks

Waffen-SS Ranks:	U.S. Army Ranks:
Reichsführer-SS (Heinrich Himmler)	No equivalent
SS-Oberstgruppenführer und General-Oberst der Waffen-SS	General-Colonel
SS-Obergruppenführer und General der Waffen-SS	General
SS-Gruppenführer und General-Leutnant der Waffen-SS	Lieutenant-General
SS-Brigadeführer und General-Major der Waffen-SS	Major-General
SS-Oberführer	Brigadier-General
SS-Standartenführer	Colonel
SS-Obersturmbannführer	Lieutenant-Colonel
SS-Sturmbannführer	Major
SS-Hauptsturmführer	Captain
SS-Obersturmführer	First Lieutenant
SS-Untersturmführer	Second Lieutenant
SS-Standarten-Oberjunker	Officer Candidate Rank
SS-Standarten-Junker	Officer Candidate Rank
SS-Junker	Officer Candidate Rank
SS-Sturmscharführer	Sergeant-Major
SS-Hauptscharführer	Master Sergeant
SS-Oberscharführer	Technical Sergeant
SS-Scharführer	Staff Sergeant
SS-Unterscharführer	Sergeant
SS-Rottenführer	Private 1st Class Corporal
SS-Sturmmann	Private 1st Class
SS-Oberschütze	Private
SS-Mann	Private

Glossary

Abschnitt	District	Geheime Staatspolizei Amt (GESTAPA)	Secret State Police Office
Abteilung	Detachment		
Abwehr	Counterespionage of the Armed Forces	Geheime Staatspolizei (GESTAPO)	Secret State Police
Admiral	Admiral	General	General
Allgemeine-SS	General SS	General der Flieger	General of the Airforce
Amt	Office	General-Leutnant	Lieutenant General
Armee	Army	General-Major	Major General
Artillerie	Artillery	General-Oberst	General of the Army (General-Colonel)
Aufklärungs-Abteilung	Reconnaissance Detachment		
Ausbildungs und Ersatz	Training and Replacement	Generalfeld Marschall	General Field Marshal
Batallion	Battalion	Grenzpolizei	Border Police
Batterie	Battery	Gross Admiral	Grand Admiral
Befehlshaber	Senior Commander	Hauptamt	Main Office
Blutfahne	Blood Banner	Hauptmann	Captain
Blutorden	Blood Order	Heeresgruppe	Army Group
der Reserve	Reserve Rank	Hitlerjugend	Hitler Youth
Deutsche Arbeiter-Partei (DAP)	German Workers Party (Early NSDAP)	Höhere SS und Polizeiführer (HSSPF)	Higher SS and Police Leader
Deutsche Arbeitsfront (DAF)	German Labor Front	Infanterie	Infantry
Deutschland Erwache	Germany Awake	Inspekteur	Inspector
Dienststelle Ribbentrop	Ribbentrop Bureau	Jagdgeschwader	Fighter Group (Airforce)
Ehrendegen	SS-Honor Sword	Jagdverbände	Hunting Unit's
Ehrenwinkel	Chevron for the old guard of the NSDAP	Jungvolk	Young People (Pre-Hitler Youth)
		Junkerschule	Officer Candidate School
Einsatzgruppen	Action Groups	Kampfgeschwader	Bomber Group (Airforce)
Fähnrich	Officer Candidate	Kampfgruppe	Battle Group
Feldpolizei	Field Police	Kavallerie	Cavalry
Flak	Anti Aircraft	Kompanie	Company
Freikorps	Free Corps	Korps	Corps
Freiwillige	Volunteer	Kradschützen	Motorcycle
Freundkreis Heinrich Himmler	Circle of friends of Heinrich Himmler	Kreis	Province
		Kriminalpolizei (KRIPO)	Criminal Police
Führer	Leader	Landespolizei	Land Police
Führungshauptamt	Main Operational Office	Leichte	Light
Gau	Largest NSDAP Area Designation	Leutnant	Second Lieutenant
		Luftflotte	Section of the Airforce
Gauleiter	Highest NSDAP Area Leader	Luftschutz	Aerial Protection

Luftwaffe	Airforce	Reichssicherheitshauptamt (RSHA)	Reich Security Main Office
Major	Major		
Musikzug, Musikkorps	Band, Larger band	Reichssportsabziechen	Reich Sport Badge
Nachrichten	Signals	Reichstag	Parliament
NSDAP	Nazi Party	Reichswehr	Weimar Republic Army
Oberabschnitt	Main District	SA-Sportsabzeichen	SA Sport Badge
Oberkommando des Heeres (OKH)	High Command of the Army	Schutzpolizei (SCHUPO)	Ordinary Police
		Schutzstaffel (SS)	Protection Squad
Oberkommando der Wehrmacht (OKW)	High Command of the Armed Forces	Schwere	Heavy
		Schützpolizei	Protection Police
Oberleutnant	First Lieutenant	Selbschutz	Self Defence
Oberst	Colonel	Sicherheitsdienst (SD)	Security Service
Oberstleutnant	Lieutenant Colonel	Sicherheitspolizei (SIPO)	Security Police
Oberst SA Führung	High Command of the SA	SS und Polizeiführer (SSPF)	SS and Police Leader
Ordnungspolizei (ORPO)	Order Police	Stab	Staff
Panzer	Armor (Tank)	Stabsführer	Staff Officer (General-SS)
Panzergrenadier	Armored Infantry	Stabswache	NSDAP Guard Detachment
Panzer-Brigade	Armored Battalion	Stahlhelm	Steel Helmet (Veteran Group of WW I)
Panzer-Jäger	Anti Tank		
Personalhauptamt	Personnel Main Office	Standarte	Regiment (General-SS)
Pionier	Engineer	Sturm	Company (General-SS)
Polizei	Police	Sturmabteilung (SA)	Storm Troops
Rasse und Siedlungshauptamt (RuSHA)	Race and Settlement Main Office	Sturmbann	Battalion (General-SS)
		Sturmgeschütz	Assault Gun
Reichsarbeitsdienst (RAD)	State Labor Service	Totenkopf	Death's Head
Reichsführer-SS	Reich Leader of the SS	Totenkopf Ring	Death's Head Ring
Reichsjugendleiter	Reich Youth Leader	Verfügungstruppe (SS-VT)	Special Purpose Troops
Reichsleiter	Reich Leader (Highest NSDAP rank)	Volksdeutsche	Ethnic Germans
		Waffen-SS	Armed SS
Reichsmarschall	Reich Marshal (Hermann Göring)	Wehrkreis	Defense District
Reichsreitersportsabzeichen	Reich Riding Sport Badge	Wehrmacht (Heer)	Armed Forces (Army)
		Zug	Platoon

Bibliography

Private research collections, private archives, correspondence and conversations

Patrick Agte	Martin Månsson
A.Althoff	Tommy Natedal
LB	Holger Thor Nielsen
Frank DeLagio	Marc Rikmenspoel
Christian Habisohn	Erik Rundkvist
Herrmann Historica München	Richard Rydén
David Irving	Anders Skötte
Patrick Johnson	Steve Tashik
Arno Kersten	Neill Thomson
Henrik Lindberg	Jürgen Weiner
Jess T. Lukens	Lennart Westberg
MIHAG-CH	Mark C. Yerger
John P. Moore	Geir Brenden

Pre-1945 Documentation

SS-Personal files

Erich von dem Bach	Heinrich Müller
Léon Degrelle	Otto Paetsch
Werner Grothmann	Joachim Peiper
Reinhard Heydrich	Rudolf von Ribbentrop
Heinrich Himmler	Sven Rydén
Dr. Ernst Kaltenbrunner	Georg Schönberger
Walter Krüger	Bruno Streckenbach
Karl Leiner	Michael Wittmann
Heinz Macher	Max Wünsche

"*Dienstalterliste der Schutzstaffel der NSDAP*" issues of 1934 and 1939.

"*Kriegstagebuch II./SS-Panzer-Regiment 12 Hitlerjugend*" 6/6-1944 – 29/8-1944.

Published material

Agte, Patrick *"Michael Wittmann und die Tiger der Leibstandarte SS Adolf Hitler"* Deutsche Verlagesellschaft Rosenheim 1995.

Agte, Patrick *"Jochen Peiper – Kommandeur Panzerregiment Leibstandarte"* Kurt Vownickel Verlag KG 1998.

Angolia, LTC (Ret.) John R. (Assisted by Cook, Stan) *"Cloth In-signia of the SS"* Roger James Bender Publishing 1989.

Bender, Roger James and Cook, Stan *"Uniforms, Organization & History of the Leibstandarte SS Adolf Hitler"* Volume 1 Roger James Bender Publishing 1994.

Bender, Roger James and Taylor, Hugh Page *"Uniforms, Organization and History of the Waffen-SS"* Volumes 1, 2 and 5 Roger James Bender Publishing 1970-1982.

Bullock, Alan *"Hitler – En studie i tyranni"* Rabén Prisma Förlag 1995.

Irving, David *"Göring"* Legenda 1989.

Kersten, Felix *"Samtal med Himmler: Minnen från Tredje Riket 1939-1945"* Ljus 1947.

Krätschmer, Ernst-Günther *"Die Ritterkreuzträger der Waffen-SS"* KW Schütz Verlag 1982.

Reynolds, Michael *"The Devil's Adjutant – Jochen Peiper Panzer Leader"* Spellmount 1995.

Rikmenspoel, Marc *"Soldiers of the Waffen-SS - Many Nations One Motto"* J.J Fedorowicz Publishing 1999.

Sandström, Allan *"Attentatet mot Hitler"* Bokförlaget Libris Örebro 1988.

Taylor, Hugh Page *"Die Germanische SS 1940-1945"* Podzun Pallas Verlag 1994.

Time Life Books *"Tredje Riket"* selected parts from following vol-umes: *"SS"*, *"Den inre kretsen"*, *"Ockupation och förtryck"* and *"Det dolda kriget."* Swedish Edition published by Bokorama 1993.

Yerger, Mark C. *"Allgemeine-SS – The Commanders, Units and Leaders of the General SS"* Schiffer Publishing Ltd 1997.

Yerger, Mark C. *"SS-Sturmbannführer Ernst-August Krag – Holder of the Knight's Cross with Oak Leaves Kommandeur, SS-Sturmgeschützabteilung 2 und SS-Panzer-Aufklärungsabteilung 2 Das Reich"* Schiffer Publishing Ltd. 1996.

Yerger, Mark C. *"Images of the Waffen-SS – A Photo Chronicle of Germany's Elite Troops"* Schiffer Publishing Ltd. 1996.

Yerger, Mark C. *"Waffen-SS Commanders – The Army, Corps and Divisional Leaders of a Legend Augsberger to Kreutz"* Schiffer Publishing Ltd. 1997.

Yerger, Mark C. *"Waffen-SS Commanders – The Army, Corps and Divisional Leaders of a Legend Krüger to Zimmermann"* Schiffer Publishing Ltd. 1999.

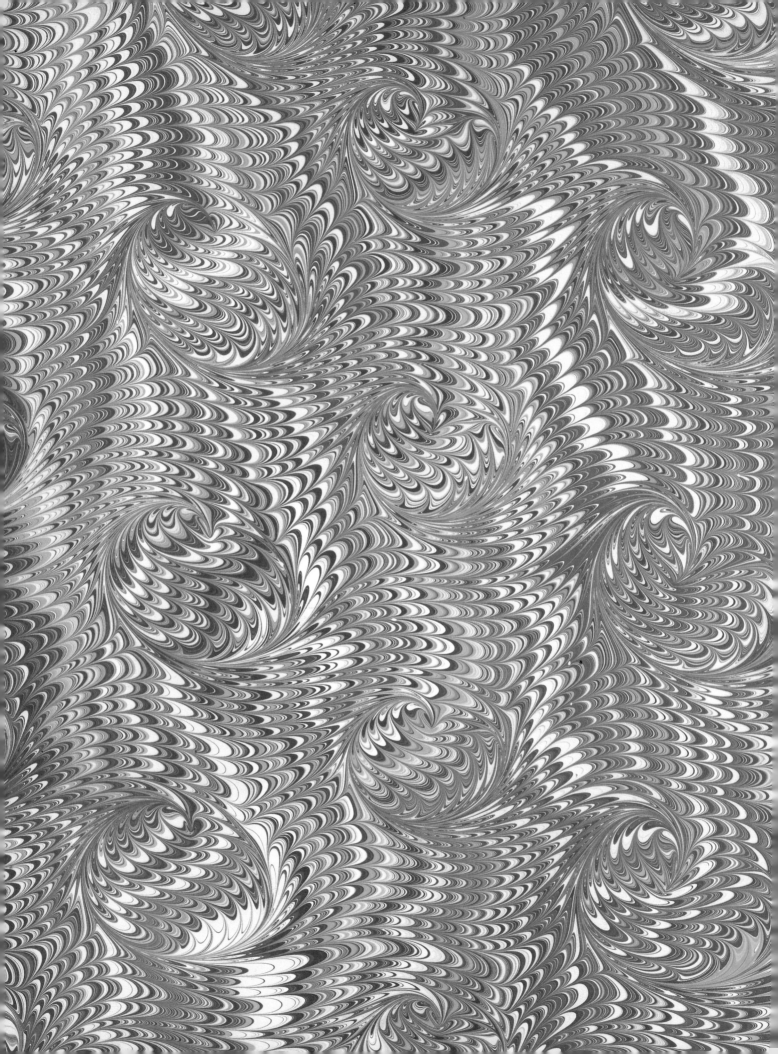